Tench

Tench

Len Head

The Crowood Press

First published in 1986 by
THE CROWOOD PRESS
Crowood House,
Ramsbury, Marlborough,
Wiltshire SN8 2HE

Reprinted 1989
© Len Head 1986

British Library Cataloguing in Publication Data

Head, Len
Tench.
1.   Tench fishing
I.   Title
799.1′752   SH691.T4

ISBN 0-946284-72-5

Dedicated to Joan, Caroline, Denise, and Julie.

Picture Credits

Black and white
Angler's Mail: page 194
Angling Times: pages 186, 198
Joe Darville: page 196
Len Head: pages 50, 59, 68, 73, 82, 96, 97, 102, 173, 179, 180, 189, 203
Rod Hutchinson: page 159
Pete Jackson: pages 55, 115
Alan Smith: pages 28, 66
Paul Snepp: page 51
Erik Thorsen: pages 21, 24
All others are by John Holden

Colour
Arthur Russell: plate 6
All others are by Len Head and John Holden

The line drawings are by Len Head

Typeset by Alacrity Phototypesetters, Weston-super-Mare
Printed in Great Britain by Butler & Tanner Ltd, Frome

CONTENTS

Acknowledgements

I am grateful to the friends and acquaintances who provided photographs of particularly interesting tench, and to my correspondents in Europe who provided valuable information about tench fishing in their countries – in particular Tom Ostlund in Sweden, Erik Thorsen in Denmark, Jurgen Plomann in East Germany, Tom Kroupa and Pavel Blahak in Czechoslovakia, Arie Sederel in Holland, and Henri Limouzin in France. Also to Frazer Simpson for updating my knowledge on tench in Scotland.

My thanks to the Tenchfishers for providing annual tench lists, to Alan Smith, Bob Dilly and Paul Snepp for their valued comments, and to all my friends in fishing who, unwittingly, have assisted with their knowledge and companionship over the years.

Special thanks go to Jan Eggers – the Pike Ferret turned Tench Ferret on my behalf – for digging up valuable contacts and inside information about the Continental tench scene; and to John Holden, who found the patience to sit around with his cameras for pictures for the book while I failed to catch anything.

Most of all, my warmest thanks to Rod Hutchinson, Pete Jackson, Paul Harris, Alan Wilson, Joe Darville and Tony Chester for their invaluable contributions.

Preface

For a long time I dodged the opportunities of producing this book. Always I found reasons why not: there were already books on tench; the tench scene was changing, and I would wait until it stabilised; I did not have enough big tench to my credit. Most of this I realised was nonsense. There are already tench books, true, but in fishing there will always be more to say, and I do not need a string of double-figure tench to my credit to know my subject.

Not that it has been entirely without problems. When you attempt to sort the experience of the best part of a lifetime's angling and file it neatly in your brain for easier reference as you work, snippets and loose ends spill over and swill about in your mind while you work and sleep. But, as the words flow and the inbuilt file becomes less congested, the task grows easier. Now the book is finished and I confess to a feeling of relief.

In presenting this book I am aware of its limitations. It is technical in places and perhaps controversial in others. But I will not apologise, for I have done my best to convey all of my understanding of tench, as well as the accumulated specialised knowledge of my contributors.

The modern generation of anglers are, I believe, interested in all aspects of their quarry. This book, therefore, is not only about catching tench; it is also about tench, the species. I hope that in a small way it puts back into the sport of angling a little of the immense enjoyment that tench fishing has given me over many years.

LEN HEAD
March 1986

Introduction

A bungalow now stands on the place where, nearly forty years ago, I caught my first tench. I pass there often, never without thinking of that powerful, dark fish with its great lolloping fins, and the feeling in my hands of firm strength.

My fishing experience at that time had progressed no further than little stripy perch and five-inch rudd, so you will understand why that tench made such a big impression on me. The tench as a fish I had heard about – a remote, mysterious fish of weed, calm ponds and high summer which only grown-ups caught. I think it was at the moment when I slipped it back and, with a single thrust of its powerful tail, saw it disappear into the deeps, that the seed of this tench specialist was sown, though it was to be some time before the seed began to grow.

Years passed. My interest, as it does with most anglers, turned towards the various other mischiefs young males get up to. But fishing was in me, and in due course my thoughts inevitably turned again to weedy lakes, quills, frothy patches of pinhead bubbles, and tench. By this time I had four wheels instead of two, which carried me further afield than my boyhood haunts in search of first more, then bigger tench. I failed often, caught sometimes, read everything remotely concerned with my quarry. I hung on every word of tench masters like Fred J. Taylor and Frank Guttfield, devoured the gospel according to Richard Walker and Peter Stone.

Meanwhile, I had heard of the formation of a specialist group of tench men, the Tenchfishers, and when in 1967 I saw a letter in the press offering membership I immediately applied, was successful, and became a proud member. With membership came a turning-point in my career. I found myself rubbing shoulders with such stalwarts of the tench scene as John Ellis, Terry Coulson, Pete Elleray and Dick Ongley. My efforts to succeed intensified and my tally of good tench multiplied. I became assistant secretary, then honorary secretary, and for years became engrossed to the point of near-fanaticism. I all but lived with the tench.

With such single-mindedness something inevitably had to happen. In the event, Bures Lake happened, a gravel pit near enough to home for concentrated attention and at the time (the early seventies) one of the country's leading big-tench fisheries – as I duly discovered.

My approach to gravel-pit fishing and the results I achieved from Bures Lake are described in my chapter, 'Giant Tench', in Frank Guttfield's book *The Big Fish Scene*. Suffice to say that through the seventies I recorded a series of big tench and made a little bit of history with the biggest brace of tench ever taken up to that time, as well as setting a new target for the Tenchfishers with the largest fish at 8lb 2oz. I continued to fish Bures, but when I caught the same 'eight' again at last accepted that she was the biggest fish in the lake and so moved on to pastures new.

Yet, strangely, the burning desire to

succeed faded. I no longer felt the compulsion – big tench or bust. My attitude and outlook on angling in general changed. I resigned from the club and found myself, now uncommitted, fishing much more for other species – and enjoying myself more because of it. That was several years ago and, while I retain a keen interest in all things tench, I no longer specialise.

Meanwhile the tench scene changes. Tench grow to larger sizes than ever, and while before there were little more than a handful of enthusiasts the country is now abuzz with specialist big-tench fishers. Indeed, my exploits of the seventies seem insignificant when compared with those of some modern enthusiasts who have capitalised on the big tench boom. No doubt should I join them I too could cash in on the bonanza, but the fire has burnt and shows no sign of rekindling.

Even so, you cannot spend the major part of your fishing career in pursuit of a single species without learning a few wrinkles about how to catch them, and in a way I feel I have a duty to share that knowledge with others. If in doing so I help my readers to enjoy their fishing more or to be more successful, then this book will have been worth while.

THE FISH

1 · Distribution

Great Britain

Tench are believed to be one of the species which only just succeeded in colonising our waters from Continental rivers almost 10,000 years ago, before the melting of the great ice caps of the last glacial period isolated Britain from the Continental land mass. Before the rising sea caused Britain to become the British Isles, Ireland was part of the mainland and England was connected to Europe by a land bridge across what is now the English Channel. Along this connecting land bridge flowed the so-called Chillesford River, which linked our eastern river system with the Rhine, its tributaries and smaller rivers of western Europe. It was through this river system that tench were able to migrate northward from Europe to colonise our eastern waters.

Tench, being one of the warmer water species, were one of the slowest to migrate, and so they were unable to penetrate far beyond our eastern floodplain lakes and rivers, while colder-water species such as chub, dace and grayling were earlier starters and colonised areas further north and west before the flooding of the English Channel made further migrations impossible.

The eastern half of Britain is still the stronghold of this country's tench fishing, though further migrations through connected watercourses and, more particularly, stockings by anglers have ensured that the species is now much more widespread.

A perfect English tench; in fact 5lb 14oz from a Hertfordshire lake.

The further north and west the thinner the tench stocks, generally speaking. Parts of central and western Wales have relatively few, though good tench fishing is found in the south and north of that country. Scotland contained very few tench north of Dumfries-shire until quite recently but now they are found as far up as Bridge of Earn, south of Perth, in an ox-bow lake formed by the River Earn. Further south in Scotland tench waters are increasingly abundant, with Lanark Loch and the Forth and Clyde Canal holding some of the finest stocks, with individual fish caught in excess of six pounds. Modern Scots anglers appreciate the fact that a fish does not necessarily need spots in order to provide good sport and, encouraged by such merry bands as the Forth and Clyde Coarse Angling Club, tench seem sure to multiply further in the next decade.

Likewise, Devon and Cornwall, once starved of tench, now contain large numbers of excellent fisheries, though so far their tench have not achieved the large sizes seen in other parts of the country. Elsewhere in England, throughout the Midlands, the southern counties, west to

Cheshire and north to Lancashire and Yorkshire, tench are well represented, though isolated parts of some regions would benefit from an injection of stocks.

Nevertheless, our most prolific tench fisheries are to be found to the east of a line drawn from the western boundaries of Lincolnshire and south-west to Dorset, with those in the south-east, the Thames and Colne valleys, Kent, Essex, Suffolk and Norfolk providing the cream of the fishing.

Tench in Ireland   PAUL HARRIS

Ireland remained connected to the British mainland for some time after the melting of the ice, but probably became isolated before tench could migrate that far. Ireland's tench are therefore a result of

The magic day, 16 June! This is the scene on tench waters everywhere.

deliberate introductions. It is believed that both tench and carp were introduced to Ireland during the reign of James I as early as 1603, but there is more conclusive evidence that Richard Boyle, the great Earl of Cork, was responsible for stockings during 1634 and 1660. He could indeed be named as the true father of tench fishing in Ireland, although his motives for urging the stocking of tench brought from England were possibly more culinary than sporting. Stockings of this nature continued quite possibly into the 1880s and, as the tench were nearly always accompanied by carp, it is safe to assume that, as in Britain, any area that had a lake and a monastery was a recipient at some time or other of these stockings.

For the tench angler with a bit of time on his hands it could therefore be a very worthwhile exercise to visit the local library and check through the books of that time. With the aid of a good OS map it should be possible to pinpoint some of the lakes. A few of the lakes which have been traced still contain tench, but strangely all the carp seem to have died out and scientific evidence suggests that very little natural regeneration took place, hence the need for constant restocking.

It was not until 1950 that tench stockings started to take place on a more organised and planned basis and this time it was for the anglers' benefit, not the cooking pot. The main reason for this resurgence of interest in the tench was the growing number of English anglers who had started to visit Ireland on a regular basis. During the early 1950s this stocking was mainly in the River Shannon catchment and some of its associated lakes but, more important, many stew ponds were set up where conditions ideally suited the tench. Fish from these ponds were to provide the backbone of tench stockings for several years, starting around 1957.

IRISH WATERS INTO WHICH TENCH HAVE BEEN INTRODUCED SINCE 1956

(Dates of introductions in brackets)

Ballymote, Co. Sligo
Ardrea Lough (1959)
Owenmore River (1960)

Carrick on Shannon
Cartron Lough (1959)
Kiltoghert L. (1961)
Hillstreet Pond (1964)

Carrigallan Co. Leitrim
Clooncorrick L. (1958)
Town L. (1958)

Cloone, Co. Leitrim
Kiltyfea L. (1959)

Drumshanbo, Co. Leitrim
Drumgorman L. (1957)
Blackrock Pond (1964)

Clones, Co. Monaghan
L. Glear (1961)

Bailiboro, Co. Cavan
Town L. (1958, 1959)

Virginia, Co. Cavan
Lisgrey L. (1958, 1965)
Rampart R. (1963)

Clondrs, Co. Longford
Royal Canal (1958)

Mullingar, Co. Westmeath
Royal Canal (1957–67)
Sheever System (1964–7)
McEvoys L (1967)
Ballynafid (1964)

Kiltyclogher, Co. Leitrim
Deans L. (1957)

Portumna, Co. Galway
Friars Lake (1959)

Strokestown, Co. Roscommon
Black Lough (1963)
L. Lea (1963)

Botle, Co. Roscommon
L. Finn (1962)
Deerpark L. (1965)

Ballyhaunis, Co. Mayo
Eatons L. (1962)
Cloonacurry L. (1965)

Knock, Co. Mayo
Lakehill Lake (1959)

Castleblaney, Co. Monahan
Smiths L. (1959, 1962)
Malones L. (1964)

Ballinamore, Co. Leitrim
Corgar L. (1957)
Willowfield L. (1964)

Ballygar, Co. Galway
Ballagdacker L. (1965)

Ballinasloe, Co. Galway
R. Suck

Ballyconnell, Co. Cavan
Carne L. (1961)

Belturbet, Co. Cavan
Killinagher L. (1957)
Fergusons L. (1964)

Killeshandra, Co. Cavan
Green L. (1960)

Cavan, Co. Cavan
Swellen L. (1960)
Killamooney L. (1962, 1967)

Carrickmacross, Co. Monaghan
L. Na Glack (1959–64)
Monalty Pond (1960)

The water boils, the spray flies, as a tench refuses to succumb to the net.

L. Derry (1960)
Ballyhoe L. (1963, 1967)

Ballybay, Co. Monaghan
Derryvally L. (1959)

Arva, Co Cavan
Hollybank L. (1957)
Guinikin L. (1958)

L. Gowna, Co. Cavan
Bawndoora (1958–60)

Finea, Co. Cavan
Bracklagh L. (1958 onwards)

Ballyjamesduff, Co. Cavan
Cornagrow L. (1957)

Cootehill, Co. Cavan
Lisna Long L. (1957)
White Lough (1960)

Shercock, Co. Cavan
L. Muddie (1958)
Stapleton L. (1960)
Drumlon L. (1964)

Graiguenamanagh, Co. Carlow
R. Barrow (1964)

Bracklyn, Co. Westmeath
Reynella L. (1957)

Killucan, Co. Westmeath
Royal Canal (1956)

Banagher, Co. Offaly
River Shannon (1959)

Prosperous, Co. Kildare
Grand Canal (1959)

Maynooth, Co. Kildare
Royal Canal (1958)

Carlow, Co. Carlow
R. Barrow and ponds (1959, 1964)

Dunmore East, Co. Waterford
Belle L. (1959)

Cork City
The Lough (1959)

Bantry, Co. Cork
Farranmanagh L. (1965)
Failbeg L. (1965)

Macroom, Co. Cork
McCulls Pond (1964)

The list of waters which have been stocked with tench since 1956 makes very interesting reading for along with the well known and established venues there are several which surprised and a couple which amazed me. I would hazard a guess that Lakehill Lake, Knock, Co. Mayo, and Ferranmanagh Lake, Bantry, Co. Cork, are just two of the waters which have hardly, if ever, been fished since the stockings. For the ultimate out-of-the-way tench fishery, however, pride of place must go to Inishbofin Island, which is situated some ten miles off the west coast of Ireland in the Atlantic Ocean. Tench of both sexes were put into St Colemans Lake in 1971 and nearby Lough Na Braid was stocked, for some obscure reason, with all male fish. When these waters were checked in 1976 the St Colemans fish had successfully spawned and created a good colony and, whereas the all-male stock of Na Braid were still present, it is doubtful if there would be any left now – unless some charitable soul threw in a female.

Apart from stocked waters tench have colonised many other lakes throughout

This tench is beaten - but only after a spirited fight.

Ireland. With a large number of lakes connected, if not through visible waterways then by underground streams, the wandering tench has set up home in many more places than is generally realised. Few people travel to Ireland specifically for tench fishing. They are content with catching large numbers of bream and roach through the day, plus a few tench if they come along, and the early morning and late evening sessions so necessary for successful tench catches are often ignored. Waters known as having the odd tench might in fact give evidence of a healthy stock if only they were fished for at the right time.

About five years ago on a delightful warm June evening I decided to forsake the pub for a few hours on a water called White Lake in Cavan which had in the past invariably produced good catches of bream and hybrids for me. The intention was that even if I did not catch too much that evening it was a useful prebaiting session for the morning. I caught no bream that evening, but seven tench up to 5lb 12oz fell to my legered lobworm, and this from a venue that had, to everyone's knowledge, never previously produced a tench let alone a near six-pound fish. Since that day I have caught many more fish from there, mainly from three to four pounds, but I know of at least one fish over six pounds taken early one morning.

Another example of tench movements is supplied by the water which held the Irish record for many years prior to Ray Webb's 7lb 13oz fish from Lanesborough on the River Shannon. That water is Puttiaghan Lake, which in the sixties in particular was a Mecca for tench anglers. Yet, despite that, the lake cannot be found on any list of waters which have been stocked.

Tench can be found in many more Irish waters than is widely recognised, but where should the angler go who is looking for bigger, possibly record fish? For many years now the list of specimen tench

published annually by the Irish Specimen Fish Committee has shown that Lanesborough on the River Shannon is the number one place for specimens over the six pound mark. However, I think it is no coincidence that new names appearing in the list such as Lough Na Glack and Monalty Lake have also been topping the specimen bream list. The tench are generally being caught accidentally by bream anglers night-fishing and I believe that many of the current specialist anglers who have been putting time in at Lanesborough may start to look at other likely venues.

For a potential record fish I believe that the River Barrow, one of Ireland's most underrated rivers, has all the right ingredients – plenty of rich feed and good, clean, well oxygenated water – and it has already produced fish of nearly seven pounds. Yet it is rarely fished for tench, most visitors preferring to fish for its excellent bream shoals, which, incidentally, also have record-breaking potential.

Putting aside our thoughts of six pound plus fish for a moment, if a good catch of fish from three to four pounds takes your fancy then I could fill several pages with lists of such waters where this is possible. The counties of Clare, Roscommon, Leitrim, Longford, Cavan, Meath, Monaghan and Westmeath all have a good selection of such venues where good catches are taken. Local tourist organisations often produce excellent maps detailing these waters but if you have any problem getting hold of them contact the Irish Tourist Board, who will be able to supply those and quite often plenty of other information.

Irish tench fishing has not in any way reached the sophisticated level seen on

Opposite *Tench of this calibre are widespread throughout England.*

many English waters. Whilst I am sure boilies of any flavour would work, the old-fashioned worms and bread remain the top baits for big fish, with sweetcorn starting to make an impact. As more anglers visit Ireland to explore the tench fishing the record will surely be raised, possibly not to the dizzy heights it has attained in England, but at least to double figures. The fish may already have been caught and returned without any official weighing; I once witnessed an elderly angler return two tench, one of which was certainly over the record. He could not understand what all the fuss was about, for, as he calmly stated, 'I caught bigger last year.'

Perhaps he had got it right, for first-class tench fishing is not all about breaking records and topping specimen weights. For many it is the chance to fish on uncrowded waters in delightful surroundings with no noise from cars and aircraft and the resultant smelly fumes. It is also the opportunity to catch fish in perfect condition, such condition that it is hard to believe that they have ever been hooked or seen an angler before. And, who knows, with the wealth of waters available they probably haven't.

I must admit that I am one of those people, and as long as I can continue to cross the Irish Sea then I know these types of waters will be waiting.

*   *   *

Tench in Europe

Tench are widespread throughout virtually all of Europe. As would be expected they are most abundant and generally grow to larger sizes in the warmer climates of the south-east and are fewer and generally smaller in the cooler countries of Scandinavia.

SCANDINAVIA

In Finland, for example, tench are rare, not known to grow beyond about four pounds and are unimportant as an anglers' fish. In Norway, too, few waters contain them. There they grow to about six pounds in exceptional circumstances and any caught are killed upon capture but hardly ever eaten, which seems an odd fishery management policy for a species in short supply.

Tom Ostlund in Sweden tells me that tench are absent in the north of his country but abundant in the south, where they are a much-prized species and reach very large sizes indeed. All Swedish tench are returned. Dan Dellerfjord, the record holder with a fish of 10lb 3oz 6dr., and Luis Rassmussen are both noted anglers on the Swedish big-tench scene. Dan already had a fish of 9lb 11oz 14dr. to his credit which he took from the Ljunby River on lobworm, while Luis took five large tench in 1985 alone at 8lb 12oz 11dr, 8lb 3oz 11dr, 8lb 2oz, 8lb 0oz and 7lb 13oz, again all on lobs and from the same venue. Luis was perhaps a trifle unfortunate because when Dan took his record its mouth still contained the hook and broken strand of nylon Luis lost in a previous encounter. It is interesting to see that most of the large Swedish tench come from a river and not a stillwater.

The accomplished Danish angler Erik Thorsen provides details about tench in his country, where they are plentiful and grow to good sizes, with fish well over six pounds taken most seasons. Average sizes are about three pounds but large catches are sometimes made, such as fifty-four tench in six hours' fishing taken by Erik himself on lobworms from Lake Gentofte in Copenhagen. All his fish were returned, as are nearly all Danish tench, with anglers there being very conservation-conscious. In 1985 Erik caught and released a total 285

Danish enthusiast Erik Thorsen holds a lean looking but good tench.

tench up to 6lb 3oz – super tenching by any standards.

At 7lb 8oz their record fish seems well below the country's potential. Erik reckons that near-double-figure fish are realistic and considers that such fish could be taken by specialised fishing in the right places. Most Danish tench inhabit shallow waters and during hard winters up to 20 inches of ice can form, killing some tench which are found floating when the ice melts. In the early spring of 1980 Erik discovered a dead tench which was 26¾ inches long. Unfortunately it was too decomposed to weigh, but obviously it was a very big fish indeed with a length greater than that of the record from nearby Sweden.

FRANCE

French anglers seem largely indifferent about the distribution and potential of their tench. They are not a popular fish, are neglected by anglers, and no records are kept. Tench are abundant, however, and grow to large sizes, though the largest authentic fish Henri Limouzin, the French angling writer, is able to trace is one of 7lb 11oz 8dr. taken two years ago. Most of their better fish, as is the case in several European countries, are taken accidentally by carp anglers. The largest fish quoted above seems unrealistic when considering the assumed potential; indeed, one larger fish is on record, an 11lb tench taken in 1980 from Aneige, but I have been unable to uncover further evidence. There are also rumours of an enormous tench around the 20lb mark from the infamous Lake Cassein in southern France, and, although again I can find no substantiating evidence, who is to say that a water yielding such huge carp could not do the same with tench?

Gravel pits, interestingly, are said to produce the largest tench. There is a group of fisheries just the other side of the channel in Dieppe containing very large unfished-for tench, and a lake in the town of Gérardmer produces big tench every year to unspecialised tactics.

THE LOW COUNTRIES

In contrast to France the Netherlands has a wealth of enthusiastic tench fishers. Tench are widespread throughout the Netherlands, where most fishing is carried out using methods similar to traditional English tactics, laying on with lobs, maggots, and bread in the drains which criss-cross the country. Duckweed evidently can be a big problem, and one angler, Mr Van Der Vet, advocates a hook with lead strip glued to the shank so that it plops more easily through the carpet of weed. Baited with a big lob, the weighted hook does not put tench off since takes on the drop are commonplace.

Lots of Dutch lakes and ponds also contain tench. Again, fishing is by trad- itional tactics, dropping baits into weed holes, raking, cereal groundbaiting, etc. Many of the bigger fish are taken by carp anglers on potato baits.

Tench are not eaten in Holland but are returned to fight another day. Average sizes are quite low at about 2½lb though better-class fish are taken every year. Most Dutch anglers favour measuring rather than weighing their catch, and the longest fish at 24⅝ inches caught in 1965 has no accompanying weight record. At least four others have been taken longer than 24 inches. One at exactly 24 inches was weighed at only 6lb 1oz, which makes it a very slim fish for its length (a 24-inch tench could easily make double figures). Other tench an inch or two shorter are on record, with one at 22¾ inches weighing 9lb 12oz, which is more consistent with the measurements of an English tench in spawn. That particular fish was caught on 13 February 1982, and I cannot help but wonder whether the capture of such a large fish in winter aroused the same sort of controversy in Holland as did Blaber's 12½lb English fish taken in similar cir- cumstances (see page 187).

In Belgium, as in France, there is little interest and no national records are kept. Evidently tench are plentiful with fish over 20 inches in length taken annually.

WEST GERMANY

West Germany appears to have great big- tench potential. Tench are plentiful and two fish share the record at 8lb 6oz 2dr., but it seems that much larger fish are a possibility. A tench of 16lb has been mentioned, though as is frequently the case with these monster fish no further evidence is available. Another weighing 15½lb has been well documented from the Polhof Canal, not caught with rod and line but struck and killed with a weed scythe during clearing operations. Apparently that fish was not the only large tench to succumb to the weed-cutters' scythe but other weights are not known.

Even these tench are put in the shade by a reported 22-pounder caught in 1961 from 'Ostroher Swamp', said to be near Hol- stein. Most people regard this fish with scepticism. Again, no evidence can be found to corroborate it.

EAST GERMANY

An interesting situation pertains in East Germany, where anglers have rejected the catch-and-return system of fishing since it is regarded as morally and ethically objectionable, reducing the fish to a play- thing, an object of pure sporting lust. Tench are a much-prized species and widely fished for, with the condition that all fish caught are taken for the cooking pot, a practice which evidently makes their pursuit acceptable.

Tench are abundant and frequent re- stocking takes place to top up those fish taken. Their record fish at 9lb 12oz 7dr is one of the best in Europe. But Jurgen Plomann, the editor of the fishing publica- tion *Sportverlag* is a marine biologist who in the course of his scientific studies has seen tench to 14lb 5oz 7dr. Obviously there are larger tench still living in East German waters than have so far come out.

POLAND

Poland is another of the European countries where virtually all tench caught are eaten. They are reasonably abundant, and like other freshwater species are subject to annual monitoring of catches counted by tonnage for the whole country. In 1984 a total of 414 tons of inland species was taken, of which 11 tons was tench. Fish over 7lb are occasionally taken and the average weights are quoted as about 3lb 12oz. Sporadically, specimens which have grown to almost 15lb have been found, and, by the way, the Polish record, a fish of 8lb 4oz 6dr. was taken on a noodle – eat your heart out all you boilie bashers!

HUNGARY

In Hungary catch records have been kept for the past twenty years for fish caught on rod and line. Carp fishing there is more popular than tench fishing, but the cooked maize, potatoes and earthworms offered by the carpers are frequently snaffled by tench. Both species are valued as food and taken for the pot. Both are also commercially farmed for the table, and in the case of tench breeding is carried out by artificial propagation of one-summer-old spawn.

Large tench inhabit various mining lakes, one such water producing the 6lb 4oz 15dr. record as well as two others of almost equal weight. The average sizes taken are around four pounds, but it is thought some fish attain weights up to at least eleven pounds. No one has yet landed one of these giants, but my correspondent suggests that more specialised techniques would doubtless bring one or two to light.

Is there any finer way for a keen youngster to spend his time?

Young Kenneth Thorsen of Denmark follows in Dad's footsteps with this fine tench.

CZECHOSLOVAKIA

In Czechoslovakia tench are relished as food and considered superior to trout, and as in Poland they are stocked on a sort of put-and-take basis and the annual catch rate monitored. Records are carefully kept for the biggest fish too and every year since 1975 has yielded top specimens of about eight pounds though the average sizes are much lower at about two pounds. Large tench are present with double figures possible, though again lack of specialised effort has prevented any being caught.

Although eaten with relish, tench are not a particularly important angler's fish there, coming well below carp in the popularity stakes. Nearly all of Czechoslovakia's largest tench, including their record at 8lb 13oz, come from one water – Roskos Dam in East Bohemia, which not only grows good tench but fair carp too, such as one weighing 64lb 8oz caught in 1978.

SWITZERLAND

Good tench fishing is to be found in some of the lowland lakes of Switzerland, with an excellent average size at about 3¾lb. The Swiss record of 7lb 1oz 11dr. also compares well with some of her neighbouring countries.

YUGOSLAVIA

In Yugoslavia, tench are raised commercially for meat. They inhabit both rivers and stillwaters in most regions and are mostly abundant. The area around Belgrade is particularly noted not only for excellent tenching but for many other familiar species, such as carp, catfish and barbel. The same area produced the Yugoslav record, a fish of 13lb 10oz 13dr., which is also the European record and the largest fully authenticated tench documented inside Europe, though even larger fish, up to nearly eighteen pounds, are found in the USSR.

Most rod and line caught tench finish up as dinners, though that does not imply a disregard of the Yugoslav fish stocks. On the contrary, authorities in some of the provinces exercise fairly strict control over the numbers and minimim sizes of takeable tench in order to monitor the overall population. The average sizes are quite low at only about two pounds but much bigger specimens are regularly taken with individual weights of about seven pounds not at all rare. Under ideal conditions, Yugoslavians reckon their tench are able to attain weights equal to those great fish of Russia, up to eighteen pounds.

2 · Physical Characteristics

With the possible exception of leather carp it is unlikely that a tench could be confused with any other species. It is surely one of our most handsome fish, its small orange-crimson eye contrasting beautifully with the freshly lacquered appearance of its broad, dark flanks. The tench, I suppose like every other wild creature, has evolved in structure and coloration to suit its lifestyle and the environment it thrives in. Note that I said 'thrive', not grow biggest. My dictionary defines 'thrive' as to flourish, and this tench are readily able to do in most small, shallow, lowland-type silted ponds and lakes, where, however, they do not necessarily grow biggest.

A glance at the stocky yet streamlined profile of a tench with its large powerful spatular fins and huge shovel tail confirms the fish is ideally suited to forging its way deep into the thickest weedbed and to probing among the bottom layers of mud where it roots for food with the aid of two small barbules situated at each corner of the lip. Food is passed to the pharyngeal teeth in the throat for grinding and crushing before being swallowed, though inedible material taken at the same time is expelled by a forcible closing of the gill covers, which ejects water and the inedible items from the mouth.

That tench are able to bury themselves in silt should they wish to is beyond doubt, and on several occasions I have had demonstrations of just how easily they do so. I recall instances of tench plunging headlong into soft bottom silt while actually being

Poorly conditioned tench are a rarity. Most are superbly fit fish like this 4½-pounder.

played. Once, a fish buried itself so deep that I had no option but to put down the rod and wait for it to come out of its own accord, which it eventually did, though it still had a half pound of sticky ooze on it when netted.

Tench are stated to have between 87 and 120 scales along the lateral line, though there are considerable variations between those figures, depending upon the origin of the data. It is hardly likely that a scale count would ever be required for identification purposes anyway because apart from their easy recognition tench are almost unknown to hybridise.

Coloration

Most tench from most waters are coloured a deep almost blackish green on the backs, merging into a dull golden green on the flanks with milky cream on the underside. Younger tench up to about three or four years old are a translucent mid-green colour. Beyond that age the fish gradually adopt the deeper, golden green shade of adults. Fins and tail are normally a similar dark shade to the back, but with a hint of indigo blue-black, particularly the dorsal and caudal. The predominantly green coloration is no accident; in the water, amid the proximity of the silt weed and rush beds in which tench spend much of their lives they become almost invisible, merging perfectly with their murky surroundings.

Coloration does vary with location and tench which live over dark muddy bottoms are likely to be darker coloured, as are those taken from deep waters and dim light, while the flanks of many tench found in clear-water gravel pits are of a lighter golden hue, to provide camouflage against the lighter sandy shades of stone and gravel bottoms. In comparatively new pits and those which collect little debris from dying weed and leaf fall, the tench are often particularly handsome, with flanks of a brighter golden bronze – some of the most beautiful tench of all.

Sometimes it is possible to catch tench of quite contrasting shades from one water – usually large waters with a variety of depths and types of bottom. Occasional so-called vermilion tench are caught, but the name is something of a misnomer for the colour relates only to the undersides of the fish, which are indeed of a dappled vermilion shade. I have never known a water all of whose inhabitants were of the vermilion variety, but I know many where the odd fish is encountered. They are perfectly healthy tench, their coloration due no doubt to a peculiarity in pigment make-up.

The golden tench is another colour variant of our native species *Tinca tinca*. Of a golden yellow colour, usually with numbers of black freckles on fins and flanks, the strain was originally developed by German aquarists and was introduced and found its way into the wild when people disposed of unwanted fish, though there are recorded instances of deliberate stockings of these lovely fish in various lakes. Albino tench and melanistic, or near-black, tench are other oddities occasionally encountered.

Senses

SIGHT

The small eye suggests that tench do not have keen eyesight, and this is confirmed by observation and angling experience. I believe that eyesight plays a minor role in their lifestyle for upon many occasions I have watched tench apparently having the greatest difficulty in seeing objects even at very close ranges. If a food item is dropped into the water to arrive directly in front of a tench's nose, and providing the fish wants to eat it, it is usual to see vigorous gulping in the vicinity of the food, which the fish cannot see clearly enough to suck in cleanly (fish have a blind spot directly in front of their noses which partly explains this). After a few misses the food appears to be properly located and is sucked in.

Note the nostrils and line of sensory pores above them on this tench.

Stationary food items lying on the bottom are also located and sucked in with the same suck/blow uncertainty. Movement of such items certainly increases the fish's ability to locate them. A tench may pass over a static item a dozen times before a sudden movement causes it to be seen and immediately investigated.

Bright objects are more easily spotted, either moving or stationary, than those of sombre colours such as browns and blacks. I have no doubt that tench are easily able to distinguish different colours. Those at the red end of the spectrum are seen more clearly, with yellows, oranges, and reds most interesting in that order, though all light colours are seen more clearly than dark.

On many occasions I have been surprised at how little effect is produced on tench in full view by considerable movement above the water line – even waving my arms about in a deliberate attempt to scare fish rooting about in the margins not three feet from where I stood. This confirms their poor eyesight. The clearer the water the less tolerant they are, and in some crystal-clear waters they may be difficult to approach. In clear or coloured water, a shadow falling across them will prompt a very sharp exit. In any case, a wise angler will always prefer caution.

SOUND

Short-sighted tench may be, but there should be no doubt that careless noises like heavy footfalls or humping heavy tackle boxes about on the bank will be easily heard by every tench in the vicinity, though 'heard' is not a very apt term because tench feel rather than hear a sound. Water is an excellent conductor, and sound waves travel through it about five times faster than in air, causing water displacement which tench are able to feel by the system of sensory perceptors along the body. Those tench three feet from the bank which I failed to alarm by waving my arms about disappeared like a shot when I stamped my foot lightly on the ground.

SMELL, TASTE AND TOUCH

I believe that the senses of smell, taste and touch are the most important in the feed-

Northampton tench catcher, Alan Smith, admires the powerful profile of a very big fish.

ing of tench though biologically there is reason for regarding all three as a combined sense: tench taste a smell or touch. Some species have taste receptors along the body too and, although no research has been carried out on tench as far as I know, I have seen enough fish respond to a food item touching some part of their body to conclude that they too are equipped with these body taste-buds. The barbules too are very sensitive taste organs. The significance of the above points will be apparent to any tench fisher who is attempting to concoct an effective bait.

Sex

Tench are certainly the easiest of all coarse species to sex by visible means alone, though judging by the numbers of occasions

I have been asked how to identify them it seems the differences are not immediately apparent to all. Females, as befits their sex, are altogether more shapely fish than males, the body more streamlined, the fins smaller. Males are recognised by their muscular, almost craggy profile, with fins and usually the tail too markedly larger than the females'. But it is the enormous pectoral and ventral fins which really characterise the male, together with prominent elongated lumps on both sides of the lower body just above the ventrals caused by the internal male gonads (reproductive organs).

The male ventrals also have a much enlarged and thickened second ray, and

Note the enormous fins, thickened rays of the ventrals, and the large body lump above these fins of the male tench.

the tips of these fins reach and sometimes even cover the anus, whereas those of females stop well short and have no thickened ray. The tell-tale gonad lumps and oversize underslung fins are all the outward visible means needed to identify males at a glance.

The view is generally held that in any given water males outnumber females, but analysis of my own catches, numbering thousands of tench from many waters, indicates about equal numbers of both male and female, and in a few waters more females showed up than males. Nettings also nearly always produce roughly equal proportions of both sexes. I believe the misconception has arisen through the habits of males after spawning, when for perhaps a week or more they group together in certain parts of the lake,

usually on the shallows where spawning took place. These are invariably hungry fish, easily caught in numbers, with sometimes hardly a female in the catch, giving the captor the impression that males must greatly outnumber the females. Males also group before spawning, though in smaller numbers than afterwards, and I deal later with the frequent grouping of frustrated males that have failed to shed their milt. All these instances would help to create the mistaken impression of male predominance.

When these groups have dispersed it is probable that the same lake will be found to yield more or less equal numbers of both sexes in the catch. The chances of a big

female turning up amongst a group of males is by no means ruled out, but an angler intent upon big fish only may do better to switch swims to avoid the numerous males.

SPECIMEN MALES

After the first few years of life males grow much more slowly than females, and a four pound male is a specimen from most waters. The size of males caught from a water is a reasonable guide to assessing the potential maximum sizes of the faster-growing females in the same water. Various authorities have put forward different methods of assessment. I have heard the view that the largest female might be double the weight of the largest male. I tend to double the male weight then deduct a pound. For example, if I catch a six-pound

The fight of a male tench, pound for pound, arguably equals anything in fresh water.

Another example of the characteristic male ventral fins.

male I would speculate that an eleven-pound female is realistic for that water.

Not so long ago a five-pound male was an extremely rare fish indeed. Six-pounders were virtually unknown, but nowadays five-pounders and the odd six-pounder are features of every season. In the last few years males over seven pounds have been taken and the mind boggles at the thought of the potential females these waters could produce. The largest male I have been able to trace was a huge fish taken in June 1985 from a Colne Valley water by Geoff Seamer of Ruislip. His tench was 22 inches long with 16-inch girth and weighed in at 7lb 11oz – a truly colossal male. Geoff caught that fish dur-

ing his opening week's holiday when he also accounted for six females over seven pounds. Other huge males over seven pounds have fallen to Rolf Wobbeking of Oxfordshire with a 7lb 8oz fish in 1985, Curly Hatchman and Paul Snepp with fish around the same weight from a Kent lake, and Kevin Clifford with a 7lb 2oz fish from the Colne Valley in the same year.

BEHAVIOUR OF MALES

Very often the bite when a male takes the bait is a vigorous affair, the float disappearing sharply or the indicator slamming into the butt ring. I can only speculate that males feed with greater gusto or perhaps more warily – they take the bait and bolt in alarm at their own temerity. On the hook the fight of males leaves females standing for sheer power, strength and stamina – and arguably, pound for pound, most other coarse fish too. Offhand I cannot recall more than a handful of males which did not give me a tremendous scrap. Often, it is possible to identify the fish as a male long before it is actually seen, because apart from the power the fight is characterised by heavy twangs and thumps as its huge fins catch upon the taut line.

The thickset muscular body and thick tail wrist powering the shovel tail are the reasons for the turbocharged scrap, but those underslung fins play their part too, providing the male with superior man-oeuvrability. The spoon-shaped pectorals are used as brakes, enabling the fish to stop dead in its tracks even from flat out, and, assisted by the tail, to turn in its own length

An example of the smaller ventrals of the female.

and to be off again in the opposite direction before you can blink. While swimming at speed the big ventrals project stiffly out from the body, acting as stabilisers and maintaining an even keel while the male performs its tight manoeuvres.

Males will plough headlong into impossibly thick weedbeds, the rod groaning, the reel clutch buzzing in intermittent spurts as the fish thrusts further and further in, often to charge full pelt straight out the other side. Females plunge into the fringes then stop short. On many occasions, I am sure, that lost lamented monster was in reality a normal male, whose power simply got the better of the poor old angler standing there with a dazed look, his broken line fluttering in the breeze.

There are instances of hermaphrodite tench – fish which exhibit both male and

female characteristics. Otto Schindler mentions bisexuals in his book *Freshwater Fishes*, and on two occasions I have caught such fish. One, a fish of about 3½lb, was taken years ago from Gosfield Lake in Essex and possessed large male gonad lumps above the ventrals, which, however, were the small ventrals of the female and lacked the enlarged second ray. The other was a 5½lb fish from Bures Lake which exhibited all the accepted male characteristics. That fish aroused some interest because it was the largest male to come out of Bures, with the result that it was witnessed and pronounced male by half a dozen informed tench fishers. The following season it was caught again at 6lb 1oz – in spawn!

3 · Diet and Behaviour

Diet

During their first year of life young tench feed on tiny organisms such as ostracods, copepods and water fleas, graduating to larger food items as they grow. Adult fish also feed extensively on small items such as daphnia at certain times when they are most plentiful, but their diet consists mainly of bloodworms and other insect larvae, including those of larger varieties such as dragonflies, damselflies and caddis; crustaceans, such as freshwater shrimps (*Gammarus*) and waterlice (*Asellus*); and molluscs, such as pea mussels and snails.

Tench are almost entirely carnivorous, with bloodworms and *Asellus* probably the most important food on well silted waters, while on harder bottoms, especially alkaline waters, the shrimps and molluscs are the chief food source.

SNAILS

Of the snail species, I have noticed a particular abundance of *Lymnaea peregra* (the wandering snail) on many of the most prolific tench waters I have fished, while on others a tiny black variety known as the Jenkins' spire shell – which occurs in millions around marginal rushes in alkaline waters – appears to be significant, although, as in the case of the wandering snail, I have never actually seen tench eat them other than in an aquarium.

How and exactly when tench eat snails in the wild remains a mystery to me. That they do feed heavily upon them is certain because at times friends and I have caught fish which fairly rattled. That wonderful writer H. T. Sheringham, in *An Angler's Hours* published some seventy years ago, suggested that as a new tench bait snails offered 'exciting possibilities'. I for one, while accepting that tench like them, have failed dismally to catch even one tench on a freshwater snail of any description, though I did have a solitary fish on a crushed land snail and have taken several on little brown slugs. I once even baited a swim in a prolific lake with a whole bucketful of wandering snails but still found that the only tench I could catch was on flake.

FRESHWATER MUSSELS

So there is much I do not know about tench and snails. To a lesser extent the same is true of mussels. I have caught hundreds of tench on mussel flesh and am in no doubt at all that tench are very partial to them, but exactly how they eat them in the wild can really only be guessed at. The shell of an adult mussel is for one thing too large, and for another too hard for even a big tench to make a meal of. However, young mussels are obviously smaller, their shells more delicate, and more easily taken to the pharyngeal teeth, crushed and eaten. And all mussels when they die relax the muscles at the hinge of the shell so that it opens, exposing the flesh inside and rendering it

Opposite   *A mussel caught tench, safely in the mesh.*

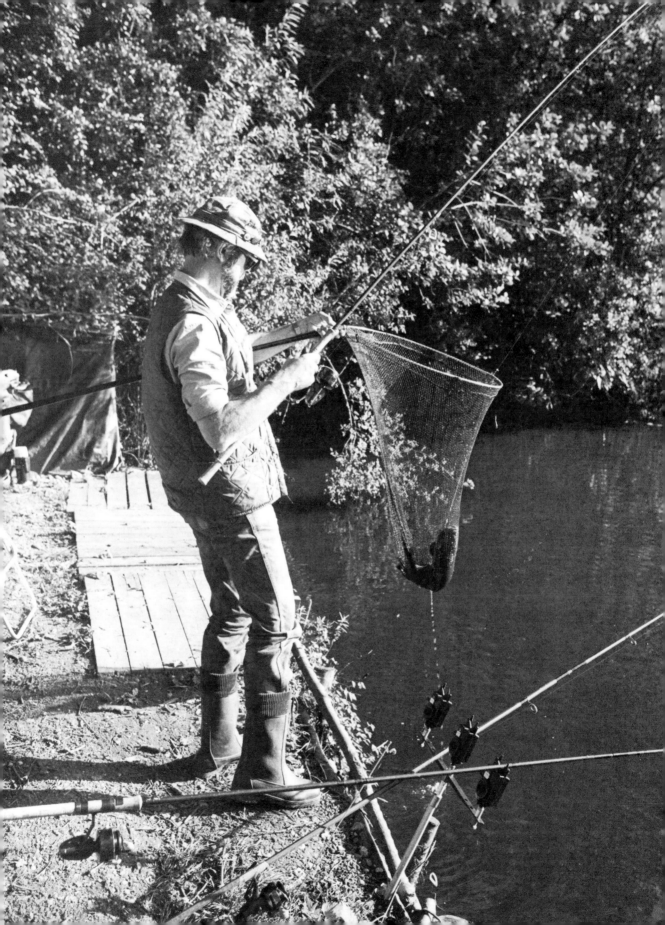

accessible. I used to keep a few mussels in my aquarium with some tench, which ignored them until one by one they died, their shells opening to expose the insides, and within a short time they were picked clean.

So tench take young tender mussels and the flesh of older ones when they die, but how can the experience of Pete Jackson be explained, who has caught tench which have regurgitated thick fragments of shell from adult mussels?

CANNIBAL TENCH

Adult tench on occasions prey upon immature fish of their own and other species. There are many known examples, in most instances coinciding with early season when there is an abundance of newly hatched fry of most species. At the time of writing there has been a hugely successful spawning of perch in a local lake resulting in thousands of 2-inch perchlings. A number of tench obviously capitalised on the additional food supply because upon capture they regurgitated partly digested perch.

That tench are cannibalistic was amply confirmed when I introduced several

1½-inch tench fry to my aquarium containing three older tench. The little fellows made their way to the bottom where two of them were immediately gulped in and swallowed. After a period in hiding those remaining were allowed to investigate their new surroundings and as one swam near to an adult the eye of the larger fish swivelled towards it watching its every movement until, within range, down the hatch it went. Aquarium experiments are necessarily of limited use, but I see no reason to doubt that similar behaviour takes place in the wild.

Behaviour

The lifestyle of tench is for the most part, that of a slow-moving reclusive lover of weed, quiet water and dark places. Tench and weed do indeed go together, and where a water contains some weed, and of course most do, tench will usually be found in close proximity to it. When not feeding they tend to lie more or less motionless at the bottom in the confines and safety of thick, soft weed. Reeded margins are also favourite resting places and to an extent feeding places too, as are the murky surroundings beneath floating lily leaves. Where there is no weed tench take advantage of any other shade and cover available, such as overhanging branches. Lakes with no weed usually have coloured water in which tench are able to get some refuge from strong light.

If you watch long enough it is common to see signs of resident tench – the weed may sway or convulse, the reeds or the lilies tremble as a tench disturbs them with its powerful fin movements. On hot sunny days tench bask on top in the middle of the thickest weed, always with their head – but, more important, their eyes, for they

This tench took maggots, perhaps the bait most closely resembling items of its natural diet.

dislike strong light – hidden below the weed. It is not at all difficult at these times for the careful boatman to approach within touching distance before with a swirl the tench is gone. Basking tench are, as far as I am concerned, uncatchable, though those resting near-motionless on the bottom among weed can often be tempted by a well presented bait.

Tench are not shoal fish in the strictest sense. Shoal fish are those which herd together in large numbers and behave more or less as one; if one moves they all move, if one feeds they all feed. Tench move about and feed more haphazardly in smaller groups, though there are many

instances of numbers of groups choosing to be in the same place at the same time, such as a baited swim. More often a group behaves quite independently of others in the water, and the fact that some tench are observed basking in the weed in one part of the lake is no reason for supposing that others will not be moving about and feeding in other areas.

Generally, individual groups are of one year class, though that year class may comprise several different groups. However, as explained elsewhere, some individuals in any one year class grow slower, and others faster, than the average for that year, so there will be variations in sizes either side of average. Naturally, where several groups of different year classes congregate together during feeding there

Watch out for the final lunge of an apparently beaten tench.

will be an even wider size range in the catch.

FEEDING

In my experience the best water temperature for feeding is 68° Fahrenheit, though tench still feed well down to 60° and up to 72°. I have caught tench in water as warm as 84° and as cold as 36°. On most waters the main feeding period is in the morning from daybreak to around mid-morning, with a shorter feeding spell in the evening as the light fails. But predicting a universal best time is a chancy business, for there are wide variations from water to water, depending upon many factors which will be discussed later. In certain waters feeding takes place in and around weed while in others groups move away from cover into more open water where they may patrol widely in their search for feeding places.

When rooting on the bottom tench tilt almost vertically, head down and tail waving, to thrust into mud or silt in search of food. Food which is visible right on the bottom, however, is approached and sucked in with only a slight tilting of the body, often followed by a curious inching crawl along the bottom, with the fish balanced on the tips of the outspread ventral and pectorals, its gill covers working vigorously as it chews on the mouthful.

BUBBLERS

Trapped air and gases in the bottom are sucked in along with the food by feeding

The swivelling eye of a caught tench appears to focus on the object nearest to it.

tench, to be expelled through the gill rakers and out through the gill covers to rise to the surface as the well-known patches of tiny tench bubbles. The so-called pinhead bubbles of tench feeding on silt are rarely confused with those emanating from other species such as bream or carp, which are fewer and larger. The different sizes of bubbles caused by each species are, I am sure, dependent upon the numbers of fine filaments on the gill rakers through which the air is sieved as it is expelled. Tench have lots of filaments, resulting in lots of tiny bubbles, sometimes covering an area as wide as a bicycle wheel. One bubbling species which can certainly be confused with tench is the crucian carp. My brother Ted and I once spent an entire week failing to catch tench which bubbled profusely all over the lake before discovering that crucians were responsible.

ROLLERS
Tench also frequently announce their presence by rolling on the surface, often with so little disturbance that unless you happen to be looking in the right place you miss it. Anglers argue whether rolling tench are in fact feeding. I am in no doubt that tench which lollop over on the surface are either feeding or are about to, and I never feel more confident about catching them. However, a surfacing tench is not always a feeder. A feeding roll is, as I say, a 'lollop', with a glimpse of dark rounded fins and flank as the fish turns over and goes down, but others slice through the surface showing the head, the dorsal, then the top lobe of the tail. These slicing tench may be merely patrolling about the lake, but the same action takes place when they are feeding upon midge pupae, which they sip in from below the surface film. When feeding upon pupae they may actually sip them in without surfacing, the only sign being a flattening of the water. As far as I can tell, slicing tench which are patrolling or feeding are impossible to tell apart.

4 · Reproduction

Spawning

There are minor inconsistencies in the available scientific literature relating to the age at which tench mature. Schaper-clause (1961) states that male German tench mature at two years and females a year later, while a Czechoslovakian paper by Vostraovsky (1965) reports four years. Huet (1960) suggests three years of age in France, stating that sexes should be sep-arated at that age in the fattening ponds to avoid excess reproduction. Kennedy and Fitzmaurice also report maturity at three years for both sexes in *The Biology of the Tench*, Tinca tinca *(L) in Irish Waters* (1970).

Despite these differences of opinion it is clear that tench mature at a relatively early age and small size. Even in really fer-tile waters it is unlikely that a three-year-old will average more than about eight or nine inches in length, and there are records of fish spawning when only 3¾ inches long, albeit in fish culture, which, admittedly, is probably far removed from conditions in the wild. Curiously enough, although I have observed tench spawning many times I have never seen such small fish spawning.

There are also different opinions on the exact water temperature at which tench spawn, and the lack of consistency suggests to me that my own observations as an angler are perhaps more relevant. For a good many years I recorded water temper-atures before and during spawning on a variety of waters, mainly because I believed that the behaviour of tench at those times could enable me to choose the most likely water to provide good fishing. As an angler and not a scientist I came to the following firm conclusions.

As temperatures rise in early summer to a level of around 66° Fahrenheit tench will be observed swimming aimlessly back-wards and forwards along and around the margins and weedbeds. Usually, they swim by tail movement only at these times, with the fins folded along the body. Since I have not observed this happening at temperat-ures below about 66° Fahrenheit I assume it to be an early pre-spawning behaviour pattern. A disproportionate number of these aimless swimmers are males.

At a temperature of 68° Fahrenheit tench of both sexes begin to display what, for want of a better description, could be called spawning foreplay, characterised by hurried restless chasing about among reed margins and weeded shallows, with fre-quent false passes when they appear to exchange abortive spawning attempts, re-verting at intervals to swimming back and forth along the margins, but faster now with all fins erect. If weather remains settled and water temperature climbs to 70° tench begin to spawn in earnest. Small groups of three or four fish, often one female accompanied by two or three males, surge into thick weed among the sheltered, shallow area selected with much convuls-ing, twisting together, splashing and dash-ing about until, deep in the thickest tangle of weed, the female releases a batch of eggs, to be fertilised by the males. They

Five nice tench - a satisfying morning's fishing.

then break away again, working their way to a nearby similar weedbed, where the process is repeated.

During the process one or more of the attendant males often vacate the female, to be replaced by others. Tench are serial spawners – that is, they do not shed all their spawn in one batch at one time – and activity is usually confined to daylight, ceasing when the water cools at night, though I have known odd instances when it continued throughout warm sultry nights. Most soft weeds seem suitable for spawning sites but where hornwort is present that seems to be selected in preference to other varieties growing in the same water. In waters where no soft weed is available I have seen spawning occur among the stems of marginal rushes, and in one other lake

amongst sparse growth of filamentous algae.

To complete the spawning cycle a prolonged period of settled summer conditions is required, not necessarily sunny weather so long as it remains warm, calm, and settled, keeping the water temperature at 70° Fahrenheit or above. If water temperature drops because of cooler weather or wind, spawning ceases; though if the drop is a slow one the fish will revert to the restless 'foreplay' type of behaviour until, below 68°, that also ceases. When and if suitable conditions return the whole behavioural pattern is repeated.

Climatic Changes

Without real proof other than pleasant memories of long hot summer days when I was a lad, it seems that our climate is slowly changing. Nowadays our springs are very much cooler in general, with winds from the northerly quarters predominating for long spells, interspersed if we are lucky with odd anticyclonic periods. Water temperatures accordingly fluctuate markedly up and down, which in turn affects the ability of tench to spawn. No sooner does a rise to the required temperature see the tench beginning to get on with the business of spawning than along comes a north-easterly cooling the water and calling a halt. The overall effect is that these days tench are obliged to spawn erratically and spasmodically, and therein lies the reason why they are observed to be apparently spawning on and off late into the summer. The latest I ever witnessed it is 27 August, but I have seen and caught tench still obviously carrying spawn as late as mid-September, at which time the chances of their completing the cycle are remote.

Early morning, placid water, and tench in the swim.

Many anglers assume tench to be spawning when in reality they are only indulging in 'foreplay', at which times it is highly probable that the water temperature will be found to be about 68° or 69° Fahrenheit. Should a season pass without 70° being reached I believe tench do not spawn at all, though foreplay behaviour suggests that they are doing so. When water temperature reaches 70° for very short periods, only a proportion of eggs will be spent coinciding with those periods, and the remaining eggs are eventually reabsorbed.

Even in a good spawning year when all the eggs have been shed it is curious that a surplus of males are often to be seen continuing with the spawning ritual, but only amongst themselves – no females. The reason is that males ripen only a small amount of milt at a time, and these are frustrated fish which have been left with a surplus which they are unable to discharge because all the females are already spent. Seeing those males one might easily conclude that the rest of the tench have also not finished spawning, which is not so.

Fecundity

Again we encounter differences in opinion in scientific literature. The balance of opinion gives the quantity of eggs carried as 175,000 per pound of female weight, but predation upon spawn is heavy. Eels are particularly partial to spawn and I have on occasion witnessed dozens on the spawning grounds, gorging themselves on the bountiful harvest. The larvae of dragonflies, beetles and other insects, diving birds and swans all account for great quantities of the eggs. Anglers also destroy vast quantities of spawn during swim-dragging operations, and it is probable that a proportion never get fertilised by the males. Add the large natural depletions by disease and eggs which fail to hatch because of unfavourable water temperatures, and it is clear why only a small percentage of the original huge numbers of eggs survive.

Hatching takes about five days in water temperatures of 68° Fahrenheit. The emergent larvae are about $\frac{1}{5}$ inch long, almost transparent, with the dull yellow of the yolk-sac still visible and a hint of dull yellow on the head and back. The eye is dark, as is a stripe extending from the eye along the centre of the body to near the tail which distinguishes the larvae clearly from other cyprinids, which lack such a stripe.

The first few days after hatching are spent hanging vertically from weeds by

This mini tench would be three to four years old.

means of adhesive glands on the head, or lying immobile close to the bottom among weed. During this time they feed mostly upon their yolk-sac. After nine or ten days the yolk-sac is absorbed and the larvae, now about ¼ inch long, begin feeding on tiny creatures such as waterfleas and copepods. At about five weeks old and over ½ inch long the fish is now recognisable as a tench, with its characteristic rounded dorsal and anal fins and almost straight posterior edge to the tail. At the base of the tail wrist is a dark blotch which remains visible for the first few years of life, though what purpose it fulfils escapes me.

Baby Tench

Much of the first few years in the life of tench remains something of an enigma for in the majority of waters these small fish are rarely taken on rod and line and rarely seen. There are several factors which at least partly explain the mystery. Because of the potentially great quantities of eggs shed by the population of tench in a water many people assume that the place must be literally swarming with tiddler tench, and cannot understand their failure to catch any. But as I have explained, the survival rates are infinitesimal and in reality there are much fewer present than thought. Those which survive spend 95 per cent of their time hidden deep in the shade and protection of thick weed growth, rarely venturing into open water and then not far, scurrying back to cover at the slightest shadow or movement. In this situation they are hardly likely to be caught since most anglers tend to fish clearings in the weed.

That said, there are occasions when young tench refuse to abide by the rules and can be caught quite regularly by ordinary angling methods. Lakes containing no pike at all and few other predators are one sort of water where tiddler tench are sometimes known to change their behaviour and become catchable, which suggests that predation is an important factor in their affinity with weed. Baby tench are also sometimes catchable in waters where pollution has produced a near wipe-out of fish stocks – perhaps because of the elimination of predators or perhaps because, under threat, the surviving population breeds more successfully than usual and produces a superabundance of young tench.

Hybrids

Tench are rather unique in their spawning habits compared with other cyprinids and, unlike them, rarely if ever hybridise with other species. Berg (1964) states that 'Tench readily interbreed with the Crucian Carp' and also mentions artificially reared hybrids with tench and roach, but of neither instance is any more data available. I think it feasible that interbreeding could conceivably occur between tench and crucians but consider it improbable that tench would hybridise with roach in the wild.

Bill Quinlan tells me of a tench he caught (twice) from Manea Pit in Cambridgeshire, a normal tench in every way except for a line of large yellowish scales, about three-eighths of an inch in diameter and very prominent, along the lateral line, rather like a linear carp. I have personally never seen a hybrid, and know of no other examples of fish which may have been other than Bill's.

5 · Growth and Longevity

For the first two or three years there is little difference in the growth rate of male and female tench. Thereafter growth accelerates, with females growing considerably faster than males. However, individual fish vary in growth rate and the fastest-growing males may well be larger than the slowest-growing females of the same age.

As growth accelerates so the body shape changes from the slim profile of early years, the flanks deepening to a greater or lesser extent, depending upon the richness

Doug Wood is a carp angler, but this 7lb tench brought a smile to his face.

of the water and the strain of resident tench. Growth varies from as little as half to as much as double the average in a given year class. For example, in a lake where the average weight of a seven-year-old is 2lb 8oz there are likely to be some individuals of the same age of as little as 1lb 4oz and as much as 5lb. No growth occurs while the tench are developing spawn, though it recommences once all the spawn has been developed, whether shed or not. Males, of course, develop relatively small amounts of milt, and how this affects growth is unclear.

Sometimes it is possible to monitor the growth rate of different year classes by the simple expedient of recording angling catches year by year until growth stops. For example, in waters where spawning is successful only in occasional years, year classes are fairly easy to define because of the wide weight gap between groups. However, in waters where successful spawning occurs nearly every year it is almost impossible to distinguish year classes except by scale readings.

Scale Reading

Age can be determined from the growth rings on the scales, the otoliths or the opercular bones, although the opercular bones are not so suitable as the other two. Otoliths can be used only if the tench is killed first, which of course in most cases is unacceptable, so we are left with scales as the best option.

It is sometimes recommended that several scales are removed for reading to allow for the possibility of regrowth scales being taken, which are useless for determining age. In the case of larger-scaled species like roach or chub the advice holds good because their scales do come adrift quite easily, subsequently to be regrown. But scales of tench are very small, firmly embedded, covered with a thick layering of mucus and rarely come adrift accidentally so that regrowths are unlikely. One or two are therefore ample, removed from the shoulder about midway between the leading dorsal edge and the lateral line. A pair of thin-pointed tweezers are just right for the job. Mucus is carefully smoothed out after removal of the scales.

Because tench scales are so small and growth rings so closely spaced they are not so easily aged as most other cyprinids. Imperfections in scale pattern can also give rise to false readings. Some researchers have found it more reliable to read the scale along the shortest axis, from the nucleus to the end which faced the fish's head. However, while annual growth rings have fewer imperfections on the short axis the reading area is much reduced, necessitating a high degree of magnification.

In any case, from an angling point of view I consider it relatively unimportant to read every scale with absolute precision. Anglers are interested in whether growth in a particular water is fast or slow, and that can be discovered by reading a scale to an accuracy of a year or two. If you caught a 5lb tench and found it to be between five and seven years old you would not need scientific exactness to conclude that it was a very fast grower and that the water was likely to hold big fish.

My friends and I therefore use the long axis for reading and we find it adequate. Scales are mounted between glass transparency slides, with one side wetted first to improve definition and help adhesion to the glass. Details such as weight, length, water, etc., are written on the slide mount. We project them onto a white wall or screen using an ordinary slide projector, which gives a large image that can be assessed by several observers at one time, allowing less chance of great inaccuracies.

Using this simple method we have examined hundreds of tench scales from a variety of waters with satisfactory results, enabling us to identify year classes and to compare age against weight in order to evaluate a water's potential to produce above-average specimens. As previously explained, growth varies considerably for a given age and this has been confirmed during scale examinations, a significant proportion of individuals weighing less or more than the average for their year class. A small number of tench from good waters exhibited remarkably fast growth. A few from Sywell Reservoir in Northants weighed around 5lb at five years of age, whereas the average age at that weight was between ten and eleven years. Whether these faster growers maintained their phenomenal growth throughout their growing period we were unable to tell.

The growth period of tench varies from water to water. Specimens from Bures Lake on the Essex–Suffolk borders appeared to stop growing at twelve years, after which age additional annual growth rings on the scales were undetectable. One of these fish in particular enabled me to prove conclusively that tench live to at least twenty-one years, and not the fourteen or fifteen years generally quoted. This tench was first caught in 1970, when it was calculated to be twelve years old and

Terry Jefferson sets up stall for a lengthy session, ensuring his landing net is placed within easy reach.

weighed 7lb 3oz. However, recaptures right up to 1979 suggested an identical age and a similar weight, showing a minimum true age of twenty-one. Of course it may have stopped growing well before its first capture in 1970, and it may have continued to live after its final capture in 1979, so it is possible that tench live even longer. I believe twenty-five years is probable.

The longest-growing tench examined was sixteen years old, a fish from Manea Pit. The fish with the longest growing period are by no means necessarily the largest because growth rate varies so much from water to water. In the case of the Manea fish the weight was only 3lb 2oz.

Tench grow and gain weight by converting food into body weight, and seasonal climatic highs and lows affect growth markedly. They feed most at water temperatures between 68° and 72° Fahrenheit and in a cool summer it is unlikely that these temperatures will be maintained for any length of time, if at all, and growth is retarded accordingly. On the other hand, a long, warm, settled summer increases the metabolic rate and longer and more frequent feeding leads to faster growth. Aquatic creatures that tench like to eat also thrive in these conditions, so there is an abundance of food for them to exploit.

In extreme cases such as the heat-wave of 1976 tench enjoy something of a bonanza. Indeed, examination of scales

shows a consistently wide growth ring
for that year.

Seasonal Temperature Effects

Anglers are in fact currently enjoying an
abundance of tench fishing as a result of
that scorchingly hot 1976 summer. Tench
were able to shed their spawn early, and
because conditions were perfect the
spawning was a highly successful one. Not
only was there a high survival rate but the
resultant fry had the whole summer in
which to feed and pack on weight and
energy to see them safely through their
first winter. Once through that first
critical winter young tench are extremely
hardy, and the effect of the bountiful food
supplies in 1976 was cumulative, ensuring a
good supply in the following few years and
enabling the fish to grow into the increased
stocks that anglers are catching today.

Some waters have benefited hugely
from that year, with lots of very large fish
now being caught. Sywell Reservoir is
one, always a good water for above-
average fish but now producing well above
form. I asked a friend, Alan Smith, who
knows Sywell better than anyone, whether
he thought 1976 was significant. This was
his reply:

Sywell is certainly producing the goods,
not only in size but also in numbers, and
yes, I do believe these new tench are the
offspring from the 1976 season. It couldn't
have happened at a better time as existing
stocks were dying out. That was reflected
in the number of people fishing Sywell –
you could count them on one hand. Prior to
1976 a typical opening to the fishing season
would coincide with quite cold winds, and
water temperatures were hardly ever at an
ideal level for long enough for good

This scale taken from a 7lb 3oz tench
caught from Bures Lake indicates an
age of twelve years.

spawning, resulting in hit-and-miss affairs
and few offspring, which explains the
decreasing numbers of tench. But spawning in 1976 was 100 per cent successful,
giving lots of fish growing on.

But coinciding with the hot weather of
1976 were the lowest water levels since the
fifties, and the acres of exposed bottom
were revitalised and as rich as any freshly
flooded pit or lake upon reflooding. What
better start for our new tenchlings? In
following years great numbers of small
tench were caught along with a few oldies,
but it was difficult to accept that they were

the same strain for the new ones were short, deep and green, with enormous fins.

Now, ten years on, these 'pondies', as we call them, have grown into a healthy stock of fish with specimens not at all uncommon, and, I think, better yet to come.

In other waters the rewards of 1976 are providing better than average fish for the water, if not quite as markedly as at Sywell. Fortunately they will continue to do so for some years, but the absence of another year like it means that when the 1976 year class dies off the waters will probably revert to normal form. In contrast, waters with an already high stock are now probably well overstocked with too high a population for the available food supply. On reflection, perhaps it is as well that we do not see too many summers like 1976. Such successful spawning every year would result in hoards of stunted fish. One such summer every ten to twelve years would do tench fishers nicely!

6 · Tench Myths

Antiquarian angling books usually dismiss tench fishing with few words. Indeed, the emphasis was more upon their culinary qualities than how to catch them. Even then the general opinion was hardly flattering, though I think William Senior (Red Spinner) was a mite strong when he quoted the following in his book *How to Angle and Where to Go*, published in 1898: 'The tench is a vile neglected fish, flabby and glutinous, bad for digestion and fit only for paupers and serfs.'

Tench the Physician

A curious old but well-known notion was the belief that the tench was the doctor fish, a physician of fishes, which had only to rub themselves against the healing balsam of mucus upon its flanks to effect a rapid cure of all ailments. Even pike were said to heal themselves thus, never dreaming of preying upon their doctor. Walton says in *The Compleat Angler*: 'The tyrant pike will not be a wolf to his physician, but forbears to devour him be he never so hungry.' H. Cholmondely Pennell, in *Pike and Coarse Fish* (1889), like other authors quotes this verse:

> The pike, fell tyrant of the liquid plain,
> With ravenous waste devours his fellow
>   train,
> Yet, howsoe'er by raging famine pined,
> The tench he spares – a medicinal kind,
> For when by wounds distrest or sore
>   disease,

> He courts the salutary fish for ease,
> Close to his scales the kind physician
>   glides,
> And sweats a healing balsam from his
>   sides.

A likely story, you say. Try this one:

A certain Gesner related an extraordinary mode of offering pike for sale. He alleges

Frequent recaptures and scale readings proved this 7lb 3oz tench to be a minimum of twenty-one years old when last caught.

An exceptionally long tench from an exceptional tench water; Paul Snepp with a 7lb 11oz fish from Johnsons Lakes in Kent.

he heard from an eye witness that a pike breast was split two inches to show its degree of fatness. If no purchasers, the pike was sewn up and returned to the pond where it was quickly healed by rubbing with a tench – ready for market next day. That account is really stretching credulity. Anyhow, we now know that pike have not the slightest respect for their doctor; indeed, some pike specialists sulk if they do not have a few little tench in their livebait bucket. And in Germany the number one bait for the biggest pike is a small tench.

I think I can explain this business of tench and pike. On two occasions I have observed instances of a pike apparently rubbing itself against the flanks of tench and on each occasion it took place while the tench were in the throes of spawning. A convulsing tench, charging to and fro among weedbeds, was shadowed by a pike, on both occasions a small one, which duplicated every twist and turn and indeed gave the appearance of rubbing itself against the flanks of the tench, which themselves seemed quite indifferent to what was going on. Strange as it may seem the spawning habits of both pike and tench are similar. Pike, of course, spawn much earlier, in February or March, but apart from that their spawning is so alike that I think it possible that they, like tench, have a surplus of failed milters which are aroused by the convulsive activities of the spawning tench. The little pike are not sick, but are males going through abortive ever-hopeful attempts to discharge their milt surplus.

More Ancient Beliefs

Our forefathers believed that tench not only affected a cure for other fish but for humans too, apparently with the ability to heal just about every ailment from the plague to ingrowing toe nails. William Senior again sums it up:

When cut up and applied to the soles of the feet his flesh will overcome the scourge of the plague ... And will cure the fiercest fevers ... When applied alive to the brow will cure head pains ... Put on the nape of the neck will cure inflammation of the eyes ... When held to the lower part of the body will cure Jaundice.

Curious indeed! One cannot but wonder how these myths originated. Some other old cures and treatments still usually regarded as myths have nevertheless stood the test of time. Have you ever walked barefoot through the snow to cure chilblains? Or seen a persistent wart drop off after administering the unlikely treatment of winding a piece of bacon rind around it? These old hand-me-downs, and others equally curious, work. As for me, I have never applied a tench live, dead, or in pieces to any part of my anatomy to cure myself of any ailment, and am going to keep an open mind until I do!

FISHERIES

7 · A Decade of Change
Locating the Giants   PETE JACKSON

How, among the thousands of waters that contain tench, can we set about finding one that holds great big specimens? Realistically, it is hardly possible to pinpoint specific waters; it is, however, possible to draw conclusions about fairly small areas to look in, after which it is really a question of intuition and having a bit of a nose for a good water.

To start with, it is worth reiterating

what fish require in order to grow big – a continuous supply of easy food, regardless of the time of year, and food which is accessible. Waters are often described as crawling with life when in fact it is the shallow margins that are super-rich. Life can be, and usually is, a lot different at the depths in which our quarry lives.

For a good number of years Len and I have looked at ways of locating really big fish, and I suppose we have managed to find a few along the way. Back in the days when we were both members of the

No trace of spawn in this 7lb 14oz late season tench for Pete Jackson.

Tenchfishers an excess of zeal took hold, and we painstakingly plotted on a map all the big tench the club had accumulated records of.

What a task! But there are none so keen as young specimen hunters. We super-imposed the data on a map of Britain showing the limestone rocks of the country. Surprise, surprise – just about all the tench fishing of any note relied upon water drained from the limestone hills. The hills of the south and south-east seem to all be chalk (Upper Cretaceous). By tremendous effort we had found yet another way of proving what freshwater biologists had been telling us for years. Looking at it that way, though, it did become possible to predict where a good water should be.

Since then I have tried to consider specific waters in the context of their surroundings – that is, the land from which their water drains – and to deduce whether or not particular sorts of surroundings gave rise to big-tench fisheries. To date I have no firm con-clusions, but I am beginning to feel that any water which is drained from agri-cultural land either is liable to be very poor from the outset in numbers of tench or will soon become so.

In the sixties I spent a great deal of time at Southall Park. The fishing there was superb, and enormous quantities of big fish were caught. It was not unusual to see twenty or more five-pound-plus fish in a weekend, and at that time a five-pounder could easily make front-page news. Then came the beginning of the end, though we did not realise it at the time. All the weed vanished and the water became loaded with algae – so much so that it built up at times to a thick crust along the dam, and ringed the reed with a blue-green coating.

Within a short period the fishery deteriorated, though some very big individual tench were caught. These appeared to have gained their extra weight by the tremendous amounts of spawn they carried, whereas previously Southall's fish carried more normal amounts.

The lake got to such a bad state that it became a source of pollution. The reason? Effluent from cowsheds and other farm waste running into the top of the lake. This state of affairs, coupled with a very reduced water level, was enough to effectively finish off this fine fishery. Perhaps the saving grace were those enormously heavy individual fish, the last of a once thriving population.

I know of a number of waters that have followed the same decline though the details have varied. Benniworth Haven in Lincolnshire and Henlow Grange, the water Frank Guttfield called Black Squir-rels, are two of the better-known examples. Though I have not fished it for years myself it would seem that Tring is following the same route to obscurity, unlikely to enter the spotlight again for many years. As in the other waters, though, there are likely to be odd survivors, monster fish like Alan Wilson's record, final stragglers from the original populations with room and food to reach great sizes.

That, though, is in the immediate future. What follows in the longer term?

In a personal list of big-fish waters are two which Len and I know particularly well, one of which, Sywell Reservoir, a few of us in the Tenchfishers studied in considerable depth.

First, Bures, which Len fished ex-tensively with such outstanding success. The remarkable thing about Bures was the longevity of its big fish, almost ten years

The moment of reckoning!

between the first and last capture of one particular seven-pound fish. These fish clung on long enough to give a good many a little bit of glory before they succumbed and Bures went the way of every other big-fish water.

All the tench waters that I know to have produced big fish seem to have one thing in common: the big fish are very much a transient population lasting only a few seasons, their eventual size depending to a great extent on the rest of the tench population dying off, or their numbers being drastically reduced in some other way.

Sywell Reservoir is a water I spent a great deal of time at, and a number of us investigated the tench and how well they were doing. A whole summer was spent weighing, measuring, and taking scales. The enthusiasm was not misplaced either, for a lot of information came from our survey. This is not the place to go very deeply into what we found out for most of it related to ordinary tench and my brief here is to discuss big ones. However, there was one item that was relevant and of great interest.

Among the mountain of scales we looked at and aged, just a few showed remarkable growth – five pounds plus in only five as against ten years or so for the rest of our sample. The fish that we examined were generally quite old and destined to die off in a very short time. That in the event was what happened. The tench fishing became almost non-existent for a few seasons and I fished elsewhere. But a couple of seasons ago it was all change and the fishing came back with a bang.

On reflection, if we had persisted there I feel that an absolutely monstrous tench could have been caught during the lean years owing to the existence of those few very fast-growing young fish. But I do like to keep the rod bent, and trying to catch one of a mere handful of fish in over a hundred acres of water would have meant a lot of fishless hours.

Even in the years I have been actively tench fishing the yardstick for a monster has changed dramatically. In 1953 a monster weighed over six pounds and a seven-pound fish was the stuff of dreams. So what is causing the increase in size that has occurred so dramatically over the last ten to twenty years? Naive as I am, I hesitate to give factual answers to this question. However, it is possible and permissible to theorise.

The waters previously mentioned all lost their fish in more or less the same way. They just seemed to die of old age and, much more important, there was practically no new stock to replace them. So where does that leave us? Somewhere along the line something is either preventing the fish spawning successfully or, if they do, then the resulting eggs or fry are not surviving to a viable size.

Pollutants of one sort or another are the most obvious source to point the finger at, probably carried in sewage effluent released into the various water courses. I am highly suspicious of the broad group of nitrates which are put on the land for farming purposes, and also of those present in treated or untreated sewage. Government double-talk has sidestepped the issue by allowing a 100 per cent increase in permitted levels – double that laid down by the World Health Organization and the EEC.

The damage done to human infants and unborn children by high levels of nitrates is well documented, and makes disquieting reading. The influence on aquatic life can be dramatic too, greatly affecting the species which live in badly afflicted waters. Algal blooms of a very high level and a lot of filamentous algae are often the result. In some cases the water is rendered almost completely devoid of life. At lower levels why should it not cause some sterility and fry mortality? If this were the case one would have the effect previously described, a water with only mature fish and few coming on.

Pesticides are at times extraordinarily damaging to fish and other aquatic life, some lingering for years travelling back and forth through the food chain. Few if any waters are without pesticides or their residues, and not many escape their introduction, not even water supply reservoirs. I well remember some years ago watching a helicopter spraying fields on the eastern side of Sywell. There was an easterly breeze blowing and one could see a fine mist drifting across the top end of the water. I don't know what the spray was, but you can bet your bottom dollar that it didn't do the water any favours.

What can pesticides do indirectly? One has only to examine the plight of predatory birds in this country to realise that these poisons kill far more creatures than they were originally designed to. The whole question of poisonous substances in water is a very complex one, far beyond the scope of this contribution, and I can only recommend that those interested get hold of books devoted to the subject.

Apart from aerial dissemination just mentioned, how can poisons get into a water, say a gravel pit or a string of pits? All poisons are insidious, crawling and creeping through the gravel until they reach open water. The hydraulic effect of fluctuating water levels does the rest. As the level of the polluted water rises above that of adjacent waters, its excess weight forces water out to balance with adjacent levels, carrying with it a proportion of poisons so that all become affected.

In a situation where a whole complex of pits is damaged, I think it likely that initially one of the pits is affected and that the damage is pushed throughout the complex. Is it a coincidence that much of the immediate countryside of the big tench pits in the Colne Valley, for example, is intensively farmed, mostly arable, generally grain crops, with all the spraying, dusting, and artificial fertiliser this involves?

From my own reading of just a small amount of the literature available on pollution and pollutants it is clear one could read and write for ever on the subject and probably still miss the vital factor which may contribute to the ability of some waters to produce monster tench. I wish I knew all the answers; I would go and catch lots of them!

To finalise: if I were to actively search for a water containing fish well in excess of ten pounds then I would look for one that was in some way out of balance, a

Shallow, sheltered and weedy - a classic overbreeding habitat of tench.

place where the tench were generally in decline. The water would occur within the limestone drainage areas of the south-east. I would search three areas: Kent (but not necessarily Johnson's): somewhere in the maze of waters west of London; and an outsider, southern Cambridgeshire.

*　　　　*　　　　*

Pete Jackson's views on limestone, agricultural drainage and high nitrate levels have, I am certain, a direct bearing on the location of big tench and on the reasons behind the phenomenal increase in tench growth over recent years. Like myself, Pete believes that the factors he outlines are not the only ones, and that not one or two but a number of fortuitous changes blend together to produce a big-tench recipe.

A glance at the accompanying annual list reveals just how dramatic the changes have been, especially when it is realised that up until 1947 only two tench over seven pounds had ever been caught in this country – and one of them was over a hundred years ago.

	7lb	8lb	9lb	10lb
1967	3	—	—	—
1968	5	1	—	—
1969	4	—	—	—
1970	2	4	—	—
1971	6	2	—	—
1972	11	—	—	—
1973	7	—	—	—
1974	9	3	—	—
1975	16	2	—	1
1976	8	4	1	—
1977	13	6	2	—
1979	26	11	2	—
1980	32	10	5	—
1981	31	12	6	3
1982	32	21	3	—
1983	32	23	10	1
1984	36	25	17	1

(Insufficient details are available for 1978 and 1985. However, 1985 produced many nine-pounders, three at ten pounds plus, an eleven-pounder, and a twelve-pounder.)

Trying to unravel this giant tench riddle is a game of speculation. I share Pete's suspicion of nitrates and their effect upon breeding stocks, not only of tench but other species too, which in many waters are seriously in decline. Most big-tench waters, as Pete says, are in decline and contain a low stock density for some reason. There are many contributory causes, apart from the thorny subject of nitrates. One is that a lot of gravel pits, due to the nature of excavation, have few or no suitable spawning shallows, so that fry recruitment is sparse. It is no coincidence that many of the waters producing very big tench are sizeable pits with few shallows. Reservoirs are also producing the goods, and here fry recruitment can also be low because receding water levels can leave spawning beds high and dry. Even where suitable spawning sites exist, our cool springs and late summers retard spawning until late in the season, and sometimes prevent it altogether, and any fry which do manage to hatch lack the sustenance of a full summer's feeding and almost certainly perish during their first winter.

As I have said, eels mop up great quantities of spawn. Where good spawning sites exist tench stocks hold their own despite predation, but where they are sparse the presence of lots of eels is a contributory cause of low stocks.

Many anglers have remarked that most

of the really big tench caught carry huge quantities of spawn – two pounds in a seven-pound fish being nothing uncommon. These fish almost invariably come from low-stock waters like Tring, the A40 pit at Oxford, Friday Lake in Hertfordshire, Southall in Bedfordshire several years back, and to a lesser extent Johnson's in Kent. I believe that Mother Nature is, in her way, attempting to redress the stock balance, for it is a natural reaction of any threatened animal to overproduce until populations regain normality.

The suggestion has also been made that the big fish are of similar length to ordinary fish, and that their weight increases are due solely to the superabundance of spawn. In some cases the view holds merit, but length is not a particularly reliable yardstick with tench. Examination of photographs of some giants, notably Alan Wilson's record, reveals that, though they are short for their weight and contain spawn, they are nevertheless massive in width, size of head, and body frame. The frame of Alan Wilson's fish was built by abundant food supplies, lots of space, and negligible competition.

One aspect of spawny tench that puzzles some anglers is the variation in weight in a fish caught several times. For example, a fish weighing 7lb 1oz on its first capture weighs 6lb 13oz on recapture shortly afterwards. It is usually assumed that the fish must have shed some spawn. But, lo and behold, it gets caught again, this time at 7lb 4oz, whereupon either the captor gets accused of having knicker elastic in his weighing scales or it is assumed that the tench has continued to develop spawn, replacing and adding to that it has spent.

However, a tench which has developed all its spawn cannot develop more, and what happens in these cases is that the existing spawn, if it remains unspent, increases in volume and in accompanying fluid, giving an increase in weight. Thus, tench which are unable to shed their spawn will weigh heavier later in the season than they do earlier on.

Tench do not, as I have heard said, develop two separate lots of spawn in a favourable spawning year.

To return to the giant tench scene. Writing in *Coarse Angler* magazine a couple of years ago, Jim Gibbinson echoed my own and Pete's thoughts by tossing into the debate the possibility that nutrient run-off entering waters from agricultural land was a contributory factor in the presence of large tench. Jim theorised that the EEC subsidies to farmers positively encouraged overuse of agrochemicals, and that the period of this overuse coincided with the big-tench boom; and, further, that nutrients entered the water table and thus affected stillwaters by accelerating eutrophication and increasing productivity.

As a follow-up to Jim's article, I plotted all the big-tench captures I knew about onto an arable distribution OS map, which confirmed what we already suspected: that most waters producing bigger tench lay adjacent to heavily farmed, mostly arable land. Very few big tench are reported from outside extensively farmed areas.

Clearly, nutrients such as nitrates and phosphates play a major role in the big-tench riddle, though I am doubtful whether they could enter waters in sufficiently large amounts to cause eutrophication via the water table. More likely they are entering by a more direct route.

Kevin Clifford, writing in the same magazine, entered the discussion by suggesting that the chief source of

Still a big tench at 6lb 5oz, but 25 years ago it would have been classed as a monster.

nutrients was treated and untreated domestic and industrial sewage effluent, rather than agriculture, adding that many of the best big-tench waters lie adjacent to, or are directly linked via inflows to, sewage rivers.

Phosphates carried in large amounts in effluent are in fact more likely to be the cause of eutrophication than nitrates, the latter having relatively little effect upon productivity. And phosphates used in farming are easily taken up in the soil, making it unlikely that very large amounts could enter waters by drainage. Both nitrate and phosphate levels have increased dramatically in rivers in recent years, but, whilst it is generally accepted that the nitrate levels result from agrochemicals, the fact that little phosphate can enter via run-off tends to confirm Kevin's view that sewage effluent is the main source.

The recipe takes shape. It appears that any water which lies amid limestone, has a low stock density because of one or all of the deterrents to spawning and fry recruitment already mentioned, and also receives nutrient run-off from agriculture or sewage, has produced, or will produce, bigger tench than normal. The ultimate size attained in individual waters no doubt depends on the extent to which they are affected. Those yielding the giants are likely to be those affected by most, or even all, of the above ingredients.

The Outlook

How long will the big-tench bonanza last? I am not so pessimistic as other writers who forecast a return to normal sizes when the present wave of big fish die off. They tend to overlook the lower weight ranges, the four-, five-, and six-pounders which are also far more abundant nowadays than they were. Providing the list of big tench ingredients stays more or less constant, I see no reason why these fish should not grow on to provide bigger tench indefinitely.

However, the nature of waters producing absolute giants probably means that their occurrence will become more sporadic. Wide gaps between year classes in these understocked places may mean long intervals before other big fish show. Exactly how long is nearly impossible to forecast. The longevity of tench in different waters varies, but where outsize tench are discovered early that water can be expected to produce the same big fish for some years before they die out. It is also possible that younger fish coming on may equal their weights before the old fish fade, giving a temporary significant increase in overall numbers. Even where old fish die off with no new fish to replace

them, other tench, in other waters, may be peaking.

It is not unreasonable to speculate that rare successful spawning years by giants could result, over a period, in the evolution of a super strain; that tench may achieve, by themselves in the wild, what fish culturists achieve by selective breeding in artificial conditions.

Meanwhile, watch out for those odd individual tench which greatly outstrip the growth of their brothers and sisters in top waters. Alan Wilson's record may appear impregnable, but one day soon some lucky or skilful angler will find himself suspending from the scales a tench which drags the needle down to fourteen or even fifteen pounds.

I originally intended to compile a much longer list of our largest tench than the one given here, but I soon realised the complexity of what had, at first, appeared a fairly uncomplicated task. In the end I have listed the country's double-figure tench only, including all documented fish, a few that were not, historical as well as modern. Even now the list is not complete, for I hear whispers of three further doubles from Kent, and two or three others from Colne Valley, all in 1985. A list of British record fish is also given.

Weight			Captor	Water	Date
lb	oz	dr.			
7	0		Mr Stacey	Pottery Pits, Weston-super-Mare	1882
7	0		Revd Alston	Ring Mere, Wretham, Norfolk	1933
7	2		B. S. Dawson	Chichester Lake, Worthing, Sussex	1948
8	8		M. Foode	Leicester Canal	1950
9	1		J. Salisbury	Eggetts Lake, Hemingford Grey	1963
10	1	2	L. Brown	Peterborough brick pit	1975
10	1	4	T. Chester	Wilstone Reservoir, Herts	1981
10	10	0	J. Darville	private pit, Herts	1984
12	8	11	A. Wilson	Wilstone Reservoir, Herts	1985

TOP TENCH LIST

Weight			Captor	Bait	Water	Date
lb	oz	dr.				
12	8	11	Alan Wilson	corn	Wilstone Reservoir	1985
12	8	0	R. Blaber	worm	River Kennet	1951
[1]12	0	0	—	—	Lake, Burnham-on-Sea	1947
[2]11	9	4	—	—	Thornville Royal	1801
[4]11	1	0	Simon Lambard	—	undisclosed Herts pit	1985
11	0	0	D. Laing	flake	Wraysbury pit	1959
[4]10	10	0	Joe Darville	worm	undisclosed Herts pit	1984
10	10	0	Dennis Kelly	maggot	Cheshire Mere	1981
[3]10	4	0	R. Francis	—	Wilstone Reservoir	1981
10	4	0	Peter Stone	—	undisclosed	1985
[4]10	3	0	Jeff Mills	corn	undisclosed Herts pit	1985
[4]10	2	8	Peter Cardozo	special	undisclosed Herts pit	1985
10	2	0	Eric Edwards	—	Oxford Water	1982
10	1	4	Tony Chester	worm	Wilstone Reservoir	1981
[2]10	1	2	Lewis Brown	worm	Peterborough brick pit	1975
10	1	0	Keith Ferguson	—	Johnson's, Kent	1985

[1] Found dead
[2] Found when pond drained
[3] Foul-hooked
[4] Believed to be the same fish

Opposite *A hard fished water, but a hair rigged bait fooled this cagey tench.*

8 · What Makes a Good Tench Fishery

Many anglers, perhaps even most, seek nothing more than a well stocked tench water giving consistent sport with fish of medium size. Others look for higher average weights, while a hard core of enthusiasts get the sulks if they are not fishing a water containing giants. That being so, the definition of a good tench water depends entirely upon the indi-

Alan Smith has caught even bigger tench, but few more handsome than this immaculate fish of 8lb 7oz.

vidual's tench-fishing philosophy.

Many factors affect the quality of fishing to be found in a water. The size and type – whether it is a gravel pit, lake, pond or reservoir – the weed growth, clarity, bottom composition, amount of spawning sites, presence of other species, the pH and mineral content, and the available food supply, amongst others, all affect the numbers and sizes of tench taken.

Small, sheltered, shallow and weedy waters are most likely to provide the

Even small ponds like this produce worthwhile sized fish.

consistent sport preferred by the first type of angler, because in that sort of environment tench are likely to reproduce successfully almost every season, yielding regular year classes and high population densities. But because of intense competition for the limited food supply large tench will be rare or unknown, and the average sizes kept low.

In an 'ideal' habitat spawning can be so successful that populations become far too dense for the available food, leading to a stock of stunted tench. But even a water containing lots of stunted tench has attractions. Stunted fish of some other species, such as roach and rudd, reach little more

than an ounce or two and are of no angling interest other than as bait or to tiddler bashers, but stunted tench can still make respectable sizes and a small lake containing lots in the ½ to 1½lb range gives excellent fun fishing.

Specimen Tench Waters

My own definition of a good tench water is one where there is a good chance of catching fish to specimen sizes, say to six or seven pounds or even more. It is possible to state with some conviction that small waters in the first category are more likely to produce lots of little tench, but waters in this second category are subject to so many variables that the issue becomes confused and cannot be described with the same conviction. Always there are odd waters scattered here and there which refuse to slot into the general pattern of characteristics of what I have come to regard as a specimen tench water, and in describing them I find myself using words like 'generally', 'often', and 'usually' with tedious monotony.

So (generally speaking!) I believe tench do best in waters of over about four acres where there is clear water, dense weed growth, limited shallows, deeper areas, irregular bottom contours, a low stock density of other species as well as of tench, and where the water has a fairly high pH with values between 7·5 and 9·0.

In Chapter 7 I have discussed in detail

Barry Waldron with a bit of Southern Comfort – a 5lb 10oz tench from Bures Lake!

waters which possess the added qualities needed to produce outsize tench, but many of the points raised apply equally to the waters now under discussion. The geographical location, subsoil and alkalinity are important issues affecting tench waters, and any having the clear weedy environment which also lie in the best geographical areas will almost certainly contain vast concentrations of the sorts of food that tench like to eat and grow big on – crustaceans, chironomid larvae, *Asellus*, caddis, daphnia, molluscs, etc.

Given these conditions the presence or otherwise of other species is a deciding factor. I have noted the presence of large numbers of eels in most, if not quite all, the big-tench waters I have known. I consider eels to be a big fish hunter's best ally, consuming vast quantities of spawn, keeping stock densities low and giving survivors more abundant food stocks and the room to utilise them to the full.

Other species such as bream, roach, crucians, and particularly carp feed on the same food chain, so the more of them there are the less food there will be for the tench. Lots of bream usually spell doom to a good tench fishery. Carp have tremendous food requirements and have even more effect on the sizes tench can attain. Carp tend to dominate a water, and tench always come off second best – food for thought for any club controlling a good tench fishery and thinking of stocking with carp.

In large areas of water the undesirable effects of other species are lessened, on huge waters even cancelled out, because here there is ample room for all competing species to grow well.

Now for the exceptions. Some waters

Opposite   Most tench anglers look for good average sizes, like these fish between 3½ and 5lb.

have produced specimen tench where the water is far from clear, in fact where visibility is mere inches and where light penetration is so low that not a single strand of weed grows. The coloured water may be caused by zooplankton, a veritable soup providing a vast and easily obtained food source upon which the tench capitalise and pack on weight. Layer Pits near Colchester in the seventies was a good example of a pea-soup water. Layer was one of the first waters to start producing seven pound plus tench with any regularity. It received regular injections of 'soup' straight from the Abberton Reservoir filter beds nearby, and peering into the water revealed a huge, heaving mass of daphnia, not in isolated spots but all over the pit. (Big tench are rare there now following an explosion of carp, which have also thinned out the daphnia.)

Sometimes a hitherto weedy lake that suddenly becomes coloured has been subject to heavy seepage of added nutrients, which encourage the growth of plankton. When and if the seepage ceases the water will probably revert to its former clarity. And yet here is a paradox: a pit in Essex which received added nutrients by direct intake of sewage had crystal-clear water and dense weed, until the input ceased – then the weed died off and the water coloured up.

Water Stability

There is no such thing as a totally stable water environment. Changes in conditions will affect the ability of any water to sustain good tench fishing. Larger waters generally are more stable than small, because conditions there may be sufficiently similar from year to year for populations to remain more or less constant. Smaller waters are subject to considerable variations in tench size and numbers, with periodical changes in food stocks, the breeding success of tench as well as of competing species, and climatic highs and lows all contributing to a greater or lesser extent to instability.

But perhaps the most illustrative examples are where there are long periods, perhaps several seasons, when tench are unable to spawn, or where an abundance of other species, eels for instance, prevents hatching or the survival of offspring. Wide gaps in year classes result in spasmodic fishing; for example, there may be a reasonable head of five-year-olds, weighing perhaps between $1\frac{1}{2}$ and 3lb, and a smaller head of older fish of specimen weights, with nothing in between. The demise of the old fish may be followed by a period when no other large fish are caught, simply because there are none to replace them until the next successful generation reaches similar weights. And of course all the other variables mean there is no guarantee that they will ever do so – some other factor may intervene to prevent it.

I have never known a small water containing specimen tench, anywhere, to remain stable beyond a few years, and for that matter few larger ones either, though, as I say, they are more reliable. Anyone hearing about one producing specimen tench would do well to cash in on the fishing while he can – tomorrow may be too late.

9 · Gravel Pits

Forty years ago it was rare to hear about good tench being caught from gravel pits, partly because there were far fewer of them, and because those that were available were notoriously hard to come to terms with and largely neglected.

Then came the Second World War and the massive demand for aggregates to rebuild the waste, resulting in the thousands of acres of water-filled holes in the ground providing much of our current superb tench fishing. Nowadays, with the rubble of the war rebuilt, the aggregates industry is busier than ever supplying an insatiable demand for sand and ballast to build new roads and motorways, factories and houses. About 2,000 acres of new pits are being excavated annually. A certain proportion are back-filled and the land reclaimed, and large holes in the ground are convenient for use as rubbish tips, and are lost to angling. But, fortunately for us, many enlightened town planners insist that as a condition of planning approval the excavation is landscaped and made available as an amenity for water sports and wildlife conservation.

We are fortunate on two counts, first because we can expect more pits to become available, and second because pits, generally, develop into some of the best tench fisheries of all.

Although excavations increased soon after the last war it was not until the early seventies that pit tench really began to be exploited. Up to then, most tench fishers concentrated on lakes and reservoirs, but as time went by and anglers became more and more sophisticated and interested in bigger fish so the better waters got overfished and overcrowded. A few anglers began to look at gravel pits for uncrowded bank space and new challenges. I was among them, and have even been flattered by being named as something of a pioneer in spurring tench enthusiasts to 'think pits', after publication of my success through the seventies. Nowadays, pits are most certainly the in waters for quality tenching.

Pit Characteristics

Some gravel pits do not give up their secrets easily, and may even demand a complete rethink if your experience relates only to lakes and reservoirs. Hard fishing some of them may be, but I have yet to fish any pit, large or small, which was not totally interesting and demanding of flexibility in approach. You may fish one, get a sackful, and be hoodwinked into believing you have pits sussed. But you find that the same methods on another leave you fishless, leaving no option but a complete shuffle and redeal of tactics.

Anglers who want to get to grips with pits should first understand the basics of the way they are made. There may be no outward signs to indicate what is below the water surface, but you may be assured that the bottom is certain to be irregular, and that the nature of the irregularities varies greatly from pit to pit, indeed

A fish is on at Chigborough Fisheries in Essex.

within one pit, depending upon the richness of the original deposits and how systematically the excavations were carried out.

Many pits are dug systematically in uniform rows from end to end, with the spoil piled in long ridges so that the bottom resembles corrugations. You cannot always see this because water covers the ridge tops, but often some of them are above or just below water level, in due course becoming overgrown with vegetation and forming long narrow islands. Isolated islands seen in pits are very often high spots in a ridge. Sometimes these ridges are interrupted along their length by gaps, a factor of some significance, as I

shall explain in due course. These systematically dug pits are the easiest to get to grips with; their contours are relatively uncomplicated and easily charted.

Others are nowhere near so easy to read. The corrugations may be criss-crossed at any angle with other ridges and gullies, and scattered with deeper holes where the excavator exploited a particularly rich seam. There may be areas of shallower, more consistent depths (plateaux), where large amounts of spoil were deposited, probably from adjacent areas of rich deposits, the digging of which leaves deeper water alongside the plateau.

Such pits are difficult enough to become familiar with, but even more difficult are those where the deposits of gravel were very irregular. The bottom of these resembles an inverted egg box, with piles of spoil of all shapes and sizes scattered here, there and everywhere with no pattern whatever, since the excavator digs only in those areas worth the trouble, leaving holes of varying depth and interspersed with random mounds and little heaps of spoil. These humps are usually easy to spot; being shallow they tend to become overgrown with scrub and reeds. Fish love them, but it is a hazardous game trying to get them out.

Pits of this latter type are not only the most difficult to chart but in my experience often the most difficult to locate fish in too. You may cast into twenty feet of water in one spot, and into six inches just a few feet to the side, and among the innumerable humps and holes it becomes very difficult indeed to pinpoint the movements of tench.

Locating Fish

Gravel pits generally contain fewer tench than natural lakes for the reasons already discussed relating to unsuccessful spawning. Older, well established and heavily silted pits are exceptions, but usually you will be fishing for fewer tench. Angling writers often describe pit tench as nomadic or wanderers. Indeed, I have described them so myself. More accurately, I believe that most pits of more than a few acres contain two types of tench – those which habitually roam around the water and others which spend most of their time living in and around normal tenchy swims, such as weedbeds, and behaving more like lake fish. The latter are by far the easiest to locate, simply by looking for the weedbeds and fishing close to them.

The former fish are a different proposition, since the formation of the bars and gullies, weedbeds, depths and wind all

A brace of beauties for the author. At 8lb 2oz and 7lb 1oz, they represented the largest brace of tench in recorded history when they were caught in 1975.

have a bearing upon where they may be found. There is no doubt that these patrolling fish use contours of the bottom as beats. Those areas not used – and they may appear little different from those that are – may be virtually devoid of fish, so one of the priorities is to discover exactly where the patrol routes are.

The problem of sorting out favoured contours may appear difficult, and on some pits it is. Sometimes you will be left with little option other than to put in the rod hours with baits placed along various shelves until success or lack of it builds up a pattern. But most pits provide short cuts, clues which narrow the odds. One clue lies in the formation of weedbeds. Given a choice of two bars, one with weed and one without, tench will use the weeded one every time. Any bar will obviously have a shelf, at the bottom of which silt in varying depth will have collected, and in the silt grows the weed. By studying the formation of these weedbeds where they reach the surface one can usually work out the line of the bar, the tops of which will be hard gravel with no weed. If you see a line of weed that stops abruptly then starts again, note the spot carefully, for it is likely to reveal a gap in the bar – one of the very best of all pit swims to fish because patrolling tench usually approach and move through the gap from both sides of the bar, a funnelling effect that produces a real hotspot. Tench frequently cross over the tops of bars but though they may pick up a bait in passing they do not usually feed there. The shelf, tight against the edges of the weedline, and the gap are the places to put the bait.

Diving birds provide more clues to what is below. Tufted ducks dive to considerable depths and you cannot tell whether they are working in two feet or twenty. Swans are limited to the stretch of their necks underwater and give a clear indication of shallow areas and the tops of bars. Coots are probably the best guide with their undignified plunges down to a maximum of about eight or ten feet and their convenient habit of diving along weeded shelves, surfacing with strands of weed in their beaks. Coots cannot stay submerged for long, so the length of time they are under provides another clue to depth.

Bubbling is another clue to watch for. Gravel pit tench produce bubbles in different ways, depending on the depth of the silt and how much gas is trapped in it.

In deeper silt, at the bottoms of gullies and holes, bubbles usually take the form of the easily recognised frothy patch characteristic of tench, while on cleaner gravel there may be only two or three bubbles, and all variations between. I have watched gravel pit tench sending up solitary bubbles on occasions, and if I had not actually seen them doing it I would not have even guessed that tench were responsible.

Rolling tench give further clues. Patrollers have a habit of sometimes surfacing directly above the feature they are following, and by piecing together sightings at various points it is possible to define the line and angle of the bar, and even which direction the tench are heading. That direction may alter with time of day, because the tench may make several pilgrimages back and forth along the same features. On one pit I fished I could almost set my watch by tench moving from left to right along the bar in front of me at daybreak, and moving back again later in the morning, surfacing and showing their direction as they did so.

Locating bars by the presence of rolling tench is of course possible only in those pits in which tench are disposed to roll, and not all pit tench do. Then again, tench may be rolling above other features, such as a plateau, but there the patterns of surfacing are irregular, with no directional sequence. Plateaux are often real hotspots in pits and it is well worth spending a lot of time locating them. In fact in the absence of any other more obvious potential areas plateaux would be my first choice of swim. I believe that patrolling tench use them as a sort of halfway house where they linger to browse and feed. Shallower plateaux are also likely to be covered with weed and are a natural choice of habitat for those tench which do not patrol. The governing factor as to whether and how much a plateau is used as a living or feeding area is the depth and its position in the pit. The ideal is a plateau from four to nine feet deep and off the northern and eastern banks of the pit.

Paradoxically, a sizeable depression may be as reliable a halfway house as a plateau, particularly where a series of bars lead into it. An isolated hole or depression in otherwise shallower areas rarely lives up to its promise; lanes are required to produce halfway houses.

Wind Effects

Desregarding the effects of wind will certainly cost you tench. I think anglers

All is quiet, and Doug Wood contemplates his next move to fool some cagey tench.

who do ignore the wind limit their pit fishing to those areas containing conventional tench swims. Most pits have them, as I have said, and if they are the only spots fished it is probable that they will produce fairly good results whatever the wind is doing. But it would be wrong to conclude that the behaviour of these tench is characteristic of those in the entire pit. Please be assured that wind – or, more specifically, undercurrents caused by wind – is an important issue in deciding where tench may be.

There are exceptions – small, sheltered waters which do not receive the full effects of a blow. Heavily weeded waters may also be excepted, even though they may be exposed, because dense submerged weed growth acts as a buffer which dissipates and negates the effect of undercurrents.

The first thing I do upon seeing a new pit is to check the reading on my compass. The area of most initial interest is the north-east corner and the north and east banks, into which the prevailing summer winds blow from the south and west. Prolonged winds piling against these banks set up strong undercurrents which move out from and along them, stirring up bottom debris and fish food into suspension.

In a really good blow large areas out from the downwind banks will be coloured by the suspended matter. That undertow causes coloured water is well known, but to what extent this happens I had not fully appreciated until one day I found myself on top of a very high bank in the north-east corner of a large clear-water pit, with a south-westerly rapidly picking up into an eventual force six or seven. As I watched, a mud slick crept slowly out into the pit, that emanating from the corner into which the wind blew the most heavily coloured, with an increasing area of gradually diminishing colour extending some seventy-five yards along the banks either side of the corner. Within two hours a massive area of stirred up silt extended a hundred yards into the pit and twice that distance along both adjacent banks.

But, long before that, carp had filtered into the area, and by early evening tench too had arrived in force, and were rolling all along the east and north banks.

Now and again someone queries the likelihood of undertows shifting so much debris, and other than doing some experimenting themselves I can only ask them to take my word that it happens. Pete Jackson and I once dropped some balls of stodgy groundbait along a ledge a few feet out from the bank of a peninsula which I was fishing. After several hours the balls had hardly begun to break up (I said they were stodgy!) and remained exactly where they had hit bottom. Then the wind changed, setting up an undertow which licked around the peninsula, strong enough to set the balls trundling along the bottom with it. A strong and prolonged wind can create a huge feeding area, in effect raked and prebaited with no help whatever from the angler. The coloured water is the attractor, the food in suspension the groundbait. Big catches can be made if you find these conditions just right. On the day when I watched the mud slick from the high-banked pit, I fished the evening session to record my best ever bag from that water, nineteen tench to 6lb 3oz in about four hours of fishing.

Warm winds from the south and west are most likely to bring on these intense feeding spells. South-east and due east summer winds can also be warm but are rarely strong enough to have great effect on water movement by the opposite west and north-west banks, though it would be unwise to dismiss prolonged winds from those quarters. Winds from the northerly quarters, although often strong enough to set up considerable undertow along the southern banks, are invariably cooler, reducing water temperature so that tench are not attracted to the same extent. However, there have been occasions when I or my friends have done well in the face of a northerly, usually during the early stages of the wind when existing warm surface water is pushed into the bank, turning under and out to create a temporary hotspot until the area cools with continued wind.

During heat-waves high water temperatures and low oxygen levels combine to put tench off the feed. We have all experienced those dog days of high summer when nothing moves. Winds have

Gravel pits provide some of the best of all tench fishing.

another effect, therefore, because a good chop on the water cools and oxygenates, encouraging fish to feed once more. Rain has a similar effect in these conditions.

Raking

In view of my comments about the attractions of coloured water you may think that I am a firm fan of swim raking. And so I am in some types of water, but not in gravel pits. Not only have I rarely known it to work but in many cases raking has ruined an otherwise productive swim for several days. Whether it will work or not depends largely upon the amount of silt on the bottom. In heavily silted swims,

raking may pay off, but in lightly silted areas and those consisting of clean gravel, it is likely to kill the swim. So will raking in really muddy areas containing lots of toxic gases, which are released when the bottom is disturbed. Raking has proved such a risky business in gravel pits that I generally play safe and leave well alone.

In a swim choked with weed there is little option but to clear a patch with a rake in order to fish at all. The swim will settle down in a few days, which is fine if you intend to fish it regularly. But with one session only it would be wiser to find an already cleared patch, or use a method allowing you to fish actually in the weed.

Clay pit tench respond better than any others to a good raking, probably because of the thick milky type of cloud a stir-up causes on a cleanish clay bottom. Foul, smelly, muddy bottoms should be left strictly alone whatever the water type.

Feeding Times

When asked for an opinion on the feeding times of pit tench my answer has to be twenty-four hours a day. By that I am not suggesting that they feed every hour of the day, only that feeding times vary so much from pit to pit, even in individual pits, that any time can be the best time. There are pits in which the tench behave just like lake fish in that they feed best just after dawn and just before dusk. In others no feeding ordinarily takes place until mid-morning,

Three died-in-the-wool tench fanatics: Rob Brace, Len Head and Pete Jackson with three fine tench from a Hertfordshire pit.

and in yet others you are wasting your time until darkness falls.

If you twist my arm, I will concede that in most pits the period from two hours after dawn is the most reliable time for feeding to begin, and it may then last until about an hour before noon. But it really is a matter of experiment on individual waters.

If you are fishing a bar and begin to get bites at, say, 7 a.m., this does not necessarily mean that tench have just started feeding, but more probably that patrolling fish have only just reached your swim. And not all pit tench come on to feed at exactly the same time, so there may be periodic spells of activity as different groups begin to feed. In many pits the best time depends solely upon which part of the water you are fishing and at what times groups of

tench happen to visit your pitch on their route. Often, you can clearly see the route that patrolling tench take. An angler gets a fish, then the angler in the next swim gets one, and so on. It pays to note the times when various anglers get bites carefully for future reference. You may, for instance, find yourself fishing a short session at a certain time of day, and it pays to know which swims are most likely to produce at that time.

Considering the dislike of strong light by tench in other waters, it is an interesting peculiarity of pits, especially large ones, that their tench seem virtually unaffected. Scorching hot bright days with not a cloud in the sky may see tench feeding hard. I can recall plenty of occasions of tench coming to the net one after another when it was so hot that I and my companions were stripped to the waist. Gaining a sun-tan whilst tenching is a strange but enjoyable experience for anyone used to lakes and ponds.

Equally strange is the preference for after-dark feeding in a few pits. One in particular springs to mind, a large pit where but for the tenacity of Pete and Janet Jackson and Ken Bingham we may never have taken big bags of tench. The rest of us, having fished all day and into early darkness, perhaps taking a few fish, would pack up and go home, or wind in and go to sleep. One night the three of them decided to sit it out right through to daybreak, resulting in a lovely sackful of fish, which began to feed only at 1 a.m., stopping again before dawn.

Weather and seasonal changes also have their effect on feeding patterns. Wind, as I have explained, may have a marked effect, and should a feeding area be created by underwater drift tench may feed heavily there whatever the time of day or night.

In the early season, the mornings, other things being equal, see the longest feeding spells and that remains so until September and October, when the late-afternoon and evening feeding gets progressively better. This progression from early to late feeding periods is explained by the cooler nights in the late season, which reduce water temperatures through the night and the following morning, discouraging feeding. But temperatures pick up during the day, creating better feeding conditions towards evening.

From about the middle of October through to early November we often get mild days with cold, clear nights, temperatures diving well before nightfall. Then the warmest period of the twenty-four hours is around noon when there may be a short feeding period. About this time of year, pits take on a glassy, cold, dead sort of appearance, easy to recognise but difficult to explain, spelling the end of worthwhile tench fishing for that summer, though the dead look is delayed in exceptionally mild weather.

10 · Reservoirs

Irrigation Reservoirs

For most anglers reservoirs suggest huge, bleak, windswept concrete bowls, but by no means all are like that. Many others are constructed for purposes other than domestic water supply – for example, farmland irrigation, particularly in fruit farms.

So a reservoir may be anything from one of half an acre for supplying crops to one of several thousand acres to supply a vast area

for domestic use. Smaller, private farm reservoirs appear in the countryside at an increasing rate, which is good news for us in cases where they have not been stocked with trout – and they very often are. Those that are not can provide superb tench fishing a few years after becoming established.

Actually, there are lots of reservoirs dotted about which have yet to be discovered by anglers. The trouble is that newer ones will not be shown on OS maps and can remain unknown. The one hitch is

Not all tench are located at long range.

that in times of drought the reservoir has to perform its fundamental purpose, which is to provide water to prevent crops drying out. So water levels drop. In reality it is rare for irrigation reservoirs to drop to really dangerous levels, partly because most contain deep areas, and also because droughts rarely last for protracted periods.

Irrigation reservoirs often provide exceptionally rich environments. Water is usually crystal-clear, weed is luxurious, and invertebrate life flourishes to give tench plenty of food. Many of these places contain few shallows so spawning may be rare or absent, and here stocks are low and the tench present grow to worthwhile sizes.

Irrigation reservoirs are constructed in two ways, either by excavating a hole to below the water table or, more often, by digging the hole then lining and sealing it with clay. Water is then provided by boreholes or abstraction from an adjacent supply. The manner of construction affects the behaviour of tench in each. In the former the bottom consists of irregular potholes and ridges, probably with deeper holes, shallower areas and steep sides, where the excavator took great mouthfuls then piled the spoil along the banks. The bottom contours are important factors in locating good tench spots in these reservoirs, which, like gravel pits, repay groundwork with depth plummets.

The second type is really a smooth-bottomed claypit, with steep banks and deep water on the shelf under the rod tip. The smooth bottom is caused by the flattening and compressing of the clay to provide a water seal, which in effect gives a virtually featureless contour. By far the most productive place to put your bait is close in on the shelf, using float tackle. If the shelf deepens to more than nine feet

before levelling, then set the float to nine feet and fish at that depth for starters, deepening or shallowing off as experiment dictates. In tench fishing, depths between five and nine feet are usually well worth looking for.

I have never found that wind – or, more specifically, underwater drift – has any effect on tench in small reservoirs, but these places are invariably exposed so wind can affect them by raising or lowering the water temperature (depending upon whether the wind is warm or cold), as well as increasing oxygen levels and triggering feeding spells during long anticyclonic conditions.

Apart from the points mentioned, weed-beds should always be considered in the selection of swims.

Water Supply Reservoirs

Big windswept reservoirs are different. I have never fished one that gave up its secrets easily and did not require a large helping of determination, single-mindedness, time and stamina.

Stamina may seem an unusual need in angling, but anyone who fished with my companions and I in the seventies at Sywell Reservoir for instance, will appreciate what I am saying. We had to make several long backbreaking trips loaded down with gear to our chosen swims, which were invariably the furthest away from our parking places on the whole water. Then fishing at all, especially in the early season, involved several hours of hard work with rakes to open a channel through the phenomenal weed growth. It was not so bad later in the season because once a spot was cleared it was relatively light work to pull the rake through it periodically to keep it clear. But I recall in

A long established reservoir in Hertford-shire; not all are bleak concrete bowls.

one year of exceptional weed growth standing in the middle of a mountainous heap of weed after over three hours' slog – and you could hardly see where the rake had been. After clearing a swim, nothing seemed more sensible to me than to collapse in a heap and have a kip under the brolly. But we had gone there to catch tench, and there was groundbait to mix and put into the swims forty yards out. It was indeed hard work.

But the rewards were always worth it. I caught my first ever five-pound tench at Sywell, where fish of that calibre came out regularly, as well as a few sixes. At that time these were exceptional tench.

Characteristics

The characteristics of big reservoirs are very much the same wherever the location. Usually they are constructed by damming the head of a valley, and some additionally have a vast concrete-sided lip extending all or part way around the perimeter to hold the water. (I have never fished for tench in a concrete bowl – most are trout fisheries anyway.) Invariably the deepest water is found along the dam, and the shallowest at the points where feeder streams enter. As the valley floods, numerous bays and peninsulas may be formed where the water follows the natural rolling topography of the valley, giving the picturesque impression that the water is long-established.

In any case, reservoirs quickly become established around the margins because of the extensive shallows in which weed can root. Newly flooded grassland provides enormous amounts of fish food well before natural enrichment takes over. Obviously newly flooded reservoirs contain no tench, except where the valley previously contained lakes, but wherever opportunities for early stocking exist it is wise to take advantage, to enable tench to capitalise on the early rich food supply.

Water levels are likely to fluctuate markedly in these huge reservoirs as well as in the small, and it may well be that those which fluctuate most will contain the lowest stock density of tench as a result of spawning beds being left high and dry. Flooded valleys will have lots of shallows

The fringes of rush margins are favourite haunts of tench.

and as water is drawn off large areas are left dry. If levels stay low, which is likely in a hot dry summer, the shallows may dry out completely, the exposed areas cracking up to resemble a lunar landscape. When that happens weed and marginal rush beds growing in the shallows are killed off and succeeding seasons see a drastic reduction in the amount of weeded margins.

Indirectly, this has a partially beneficial effect in that dried-out silty areas become overgrown and more fertile, providing very rich feeding grounds when the reservoir fills again. Such an environment may produce very large tench indeed.

LOCATION

As always, fish location is of primary importance to success. The shallow silted-up areas where feeder streams enter are consistently reliable spots, especially in the

early season, because large numbers of tench usually colonise those areas before spawning and for a period afterwards.

I well recall a lovely haul of big tench shared by Pete and Janet Jackson, Harry Green and myself in 1972 at Sywell. A feeder entered at the tip of a long arm of the reservoir, heavily silting an area extending some two hundred yards into the arm where rooted weed grew profusely. Warm, settled weather had kept the tench in the area well after spawning was finished, so we set up pitch where the bottom sloped into slightly deeper water and where the dense weed growth ended. We blockfed maggots and fished maggot on the hook, and I forget how many tench we took that day but it was in the region of thirty-odd fish, only one of which was below five pounds and some of over six.

A few days later I had moored a boat close to one side of the hot area intending to fish float tackle, with which I thought I could turn some of the innumerable twitch bites of the previous session into proper takes. But the effort coincided with a change in the weather, the wind turned, it got cooler, and in the clear water beneath the boat I was able to watch a flotilla of big tench making their way deliberately out of the shallows towards deeper water, where, over the following days, catches returned to normal.

That was a classic example of tench on the move with changes in conditions. I believe that reservoir tench behaviour is in some ways similar to that in gravel pits in that there are nearly always fish to be found in tenchy types of swims in weedy areas, while others move around according to conditions.

RAKING
Characteristic of most big reservoirs are

wide belts of marginal weed which may extend many yards into the water to where the shallows slope away into deeper water. At the top of the slope the weed stops abruptly, forming an easily definable weed wall along the fringes of which tench like to browse. These weed walls are favourite places to fish – providing you are not afraid of some hard work with the rake first. The place to put the bait is at the entrance of the raked channel, which ideally should be at least eight feet wide to provide a reasonable chance of steering a hooked tench back through it. Even then some will be lost when they bolt sideways in front of the entrance or kite into the weed walls either side of the channel.

Of course you could always make yourself a 'hedgehog'. The hedgehog is a contraption devised to lessen the task of clearing channels – an 8-foot-wide rake needing two men to lift and about six to haul ashore after it has been manhandled onto a boat, rowed to the required spot and tipped over the side. It works, too, one pull through totally clearing a channel eight feet wide.

Once the channel is cleared, regular baiting closer in will in due course encourage tench to feed at closer range, so reducing hazards. With an acceptable depth and care you can even wean them in really close.

HOTSPOTS
So weedbed fringes are good spots to head for when fishing a reservoir for the first time. With experience, you soon discover that some areas are better than others, sometimes even in open water containing little or no weed. Wind and undertows are again key issues, creating permanent or semi-permanent hotspots into which food is deposited by drift lanes. Drift lanes in

A nylon keepsack is superior to a keep-net for retaining the catch.

and hedges are often drowned when a reservoir is flooded they should be noted too. Often a visible hedge continues beneath the surface, creating a potential food larder. The next step is to explore the northern and eastern banks, which probably receive the brunt of the prevailing winds (I say probably because on some reservoir valleys there is a funnelling effect so that wind from a certain direction may be diverted – or even appear to blow outwards from the middle).

Now attempt to work out the direction of undertows out from and along the downwind shores, and visualise how the visible bank features will affect them, and thence areas where food may be deposited. Of course things are not quite so clear-cut as that, but at least you will have made a start.

If you have access to a boat and echo-sounder the next job is certainly made easier. If not, then it is a matter of splodging about with depth plummets to identify contours. I like areas between seven and twelve feet deep, preferably a depression or drop-off adjacent to an 'upstream' shallower area. If there is weed so much the better, but in the sort of spots we are looking for it does not matter if there is none at all.

The important point to remember is that tench are unlikely to be found regularly in the strongest of the underwater drift where the suspended debris is being strongly pushed along. The hotspots will be the pockets of quiet water behind, or adjacent to, obstructions to the drift, such as the lee side of peninsular continuations, basins, depressions, gaps in weedbeds, and so on – 'dustbins' where the undertow is impeded and in which food accumulates.

Spots towards the tail of the drift lanes where the undertow slows and dissipates

water are not unlike those seen on a blustery autumn day along any tree-lined street, when dead leaves and rubbish funnelled by the wind lodge and accumulate around obstructions such as the bases of tree-trunks, alleyways, corners, and so on. Imagine the dead leaves and rubbish to be fish food piling up along slopes, gathering in troughs and depressions and other bottom contours, and you get the picture of how these hotspots are created.

There are few substitutes for experience in locating hotspots, but it shortens the odds if you take a compass reading then draw up a map outlining bank profile, gradients and features. Peninsulas particularly should be noted, and since copses are in my experience the best of all to explore. This point has been emphasised in my own fishing, and friends who do more big-reservoir fishing than I do confirm my experiences. It was first brought home to me years ago on a day after big-reservoir roach. A fresh wind had blown for several days from the south-west bringing cloud and generally unsettled conditions, and I first of all chose to fish the east bank into which the wind was blowing – usually a reliable choice for the roach.

The undertow was powerful, to say the least, and I had to ballast my leger bobbins with three swan shot to counterbalance the pull. Whether it was the insensitivity of the method or an absence of roach I cannot say, but a lack of action caused me to move

further along the bank, where I found the undertow much less, needing only one swan shot for counterbalance. But again no roach, so again a move, this time yet further along the same bank.

Casting out and setting the bobbins, I immediately noticed that minimal lead was needed. It was not long before I had the first bite, resulting in not the intended roach but a tench, the first of several in the remainder of that session.

On another occasion I fished with Pete Jackson, whose rods were kept regularly bent with a string of tench while I, just twenty yards along the bank, was getting next to no action at all. Since I was using identical baits, in this case lobs, and end

Opposite This common carp fooled the author into thinking he had hooked a turbo-charged tench!

Len Head during a hectic spell!

tackle we could not figure out why, until I realised that the undertow in my swim necessitated weighting the bobbins with a swan shot, while Pete needed none at all in his.

What had happened was that we were fishing either side of a small peninsula which continued as an elongated hump into the water, dividing our swims. My swim was on the side facing the undertow, which curled over the ridge to leave an area of quiet water on the other side, into which Pete was casting. In this example the obstruction to the undercurrent was the ridge, but weed clumps, the remains of hedges, and any other feature diverting water movement has a similar effect.

All this being so, you may conclude that if you are fishing a big reservoir and find a strong undertow in your swim all you have to do is move until you find a spot where there is little or none. But, of course, there may be undercurrents between your rods and a quieter 'dustbin' area so that, although you cast into a hotspot, the drift closer in still drags the bobbins up. Pinpointing features, sighting rollers, and bites or lack of them will prove whether the swim is worth persisting with. If I spend one blank session and have no sign of tench while others are catching, then I would lose no time in moving swims.

FEEDING PATTERNS

It is a brave man who would categorically state the best feeding times on all reservoirs, because what applies on one can be way out on another. Local knowledge is invaluable if you can get it; otherwise it is a case of fish and find out.

It is just about possible to generalise broadly. Tench in small to medium reservoirs usually conform to the traditional early and late feeding times as found on most lakes, with early morning being more reliable than evening fishing. Big reservoirs are much more variable, though it is possible to say with reasonable conviction that feeding periods are longer and likely to occur later in the day. One of the good things about big waters is that it is not quite so necessary to get to the water at the crack of daybreak in order to cash in on post-dawn feeding, though that of course may be required to bag your favourite swim. It is not unusual for the indicators to remain quite motionless until mid-morning, when tench begin to feed, continuing often even in bright sunlight right through the middle of the day.

Unfortunately, though, these late feeding patterns are not universal and I can recall enough occasions when early risers had good sport while the stayabeds, expecting late feeding, went home fishless.

Night fishing on many reservoirs seems to be a waste of time, though in truth most of the larger public supply waters enforce a night ban anyway. Friends and I have on occasions fished on at various venues (for experimental and scientific purposes, of course) well into dark, sometimes all night, rarely with satisfactory results.

11 · Lakes and Rivers

Although we tench enthusiasts can rejoice at the increasing availability of pits and reservoirs, we should also feel saddened at the slowly diminishing numbers of natural lakes and ponds. Numbers of them where I used to catch tench are no more. The little lake where I caught my first ever tench became a building plot. The tiny farm pond which used to contain tench of proportions quite out of character with its size was filled in so that the pitifully small plot gained could grow a loaf more wheat.

High summer on the banks of a lovely Essex tench lake.

But there are still plenty of lakes around with good tench fishing, and I think that fishing on small lakes offers some of the most enjoyable tenching of all. Powerful rods, long-range tactics, feeder fishing and boilie hurling have little place on small lakes. That is not to say that you would catch no tench if you used those methods, but to me small lakes are all about misty tench-fisher's dawns, flat calms, frothy bubbles, and scarlet-tipped floats by lily beds.

Rivers and drains are, and always have been, very much neglected by tench fishermen. Some lowland waterways are becoming increasingly good tench habitats. As abstraction increases, flow rates decrease, and the slower the flow the more suitable the habitat for tench to flourish. The middle to lower reaches of some rivers – for example, the Great Ouse, Welland, and Suffolk Stour – and most of the drains can be likened in many ways to huge elongated mud-bottomed lakes. Summer flows are minimal; in fact, I have 'trotted' along lake undertows at a faster float speed than you could find in the middle reaches of many lowland rivers. Slow flows, enrichment by agricultural run-off and increased weed growth all contribute to increasing populations of tench. Moreover, lack of flow is likely to reduce the numbers of fast-water-loving species such as roach, dace and chub, which will decline (indeed are declining on many rivers), leaving tench along with bream and carp to fill the niche.

I am sure that in years to come tench are going to figure more and more in river, drain, and canal catches, not only in large bags but for big fish too. The inhibiting factor, as I see it, is the possibility that river temperatures may not often reach the required levels for long enough for successful spawning. I have never monitored river temperatures in high summer, being generally occupied on still waters, so am unable to say whether the necessary temperatures of about 70° Fahrenheit are reached. However, in a summer such as that of 1976 a high success rate would be likely, leading to good tench stocks for many years afterwards.

A picturesque lake, and a good tench sliding over the rim of the net: what more could a tench man ask?

Lakes

LOCATING TENCH

Most lakes were originally formed in the grounds of country farms, estates and monasteries as sporting and recreational assets or stew ponds. The characteristics are similar in each in that a natural or built-up dam contains the water provided by a feeder stream which floods the valley. In this respect most lakes are not unlike small domestic water supply reservoirs, the deepest water at the dam, the shallowest at the head of the valley where the stream enters, with gently shelving bottoms from the sides towards the middle.

A typical lake shelves up gradually from the dam to the opposite end and from the middle to the margins. Apart from that, pronounced bottom features which might

A weedy corner of a small lake, and a small but spirited tench slides over the net.

help in locating tench are rare – there are normally no bars or gullies as such. There is sometimes a channel where a stream once flowed, probably running down the centre of the lake towards the middle of the dam – an obvious feature to search for if it is still there. But in old-established lakes it is likely that the original stream bed has silted up and levelled off.

Even where it has levelled off in the main lake, the inflowing stream at the head may, if strong enough, continue as a channel for some way into the shallows. That channel may be surprisingly deep, certainly deep enough for tench to funnel up from the main lake, and here they are catchable even though the surrounding bottom is but inches deep. Weedbed formation gives a visible clue in locating these underwater streams because, although the entire shallows out from the mouth of the feeder will probably be covered, weed grows just a little bit more thinly or is absent in the actual stream bed. In one estate lake I know the stream bed is clearly defined because the weed is of a slightly fresher green colouring than elsewhere, presumably due to the continuous flow of the feeder through the channel. It is strange that tench seek areas out of the current in rivers, yet are often attracted to moving water in lakes.

Weedbeds provide the basis of swim location in most natural lakes. The soft muddy bottoms and large areas of shallows around the margins mean that growth is profuse, and in lakes with no really deep areas weed may cover the entire area. Smaller lakes are generally shallowest and so more prone to 100 per cent weed cover, while larger lakes more often contain areas in the middle and in the dam area deep enough to deter thick growth. Tench have an affinity with weed in any water but never more so than in soft-bottomed lakes. The behaviour of lake fish differs in several ways, which can also aid swim selection. They are particularly sensitive to light intensity – much more so than pit and reservoir fish – and water temperature is another important consideration. Moreover, lake fish do not move around to the same extent as those in other types of water.

Huge lakes may be an exception to these generalisations, and there big-pit and reservoir tactics may be more appropriate, but for every lake over about ten acres there are probably a hundred under, so I think my comments apply to the vast majority.

LIGHT INTENSITY

Their dislike of strong light means that tench spend most of their time hidden deep inside weedbeds, venturing out into holes and clearings to feed only at times of subdued light, such as the early morning, late evening, or when heavy cloud cover reduces light levels during the day. Of course, all tench anglers know that. Or do they? Perhaps not, for it is a common sight to see anglers turning up long after the fish have stopped feeding in the open and retired to the weedbeds. In fact tench could still be caught, simply by fishing slap in the middle of the weed, but more of that later.

Natural gaps or clearings in weedbeds are classic productive lake swims, especially if the depth is between four and eight feet. Swims on the east bank are more often than not a better proposition for morning sessions, not because tench move there to feed, or even feed better, but because the sun will rise behind you, giving a longer period of low shadow in the swim so that fish feed longer. High trees behind the pitch extend low light levels longer still.

Evening sessions may be better spent on the west bank, behind which the sun dips – for similar reasons. I have found that lakes have best morning banks and best evening banks and attach some importance to the position of the sun when selecting swims. Except on overcast days the feeding spells are usually of short duration, a few hours in the morning and a shorter spell in the evening, so it pays to take any possible advantage of bank features which reduce light, thus extending the feeding period.

In the late season the sun angles are lower, and this needs to be taken into account. Cloudy days cancel out the strategy anyway, because then tench may feed all day and anywhere.

WATER TEMPERATURE

This can be important at any time, particularly in the early season. It affects fish behaviour, and therefore the selection of a swim. There will be a migration towards the shallows as temperatures climb towards spawning levels. Males are first to arrive, with females following. It has been fashionable for anglers to scoff at the value of monitoring water temperatures, and in some waters, at some times, they have a point. After all, one is hardly likely to call off a day's fishing just because water temperature is not 100 per cent favourable. But towards spawning time you can really plan strategy according to a thermometer reading. The tench of Bures Lake a few years back provided a good illustration.

It was early July and although tench had not yet spawned there were numbers gathered in the shallows, where good bags had been taken from the opening of the season. A warmer spell of weather had settled in, and when I arrived at daybreak the first thing I did was to check the water temperature in the shallows, where I found it to be 68° Fahrenheit. With a hot day imminent, I reasoned that it would soon reach 69° or 70°, and those tench in the shallows would be more interested in breeding than feeding, so I headed for deeper water.

Every swim on the shallows was soon occupied, yet the only tench to come out that morning were to my rods. Those

fishing on the shallows had swims full of tench indulging in their pre-spawning ritual, refusing to pick up a single bait. There are far fewer tench in the deeps at these times, but those that are there are catchable. I choose deep water whenever I suspect tench may be beginning to spawn, and you can predict when and even where by thermometer readings.

At other times you do not have to stick the thermometer into the water to know that its temperature may affect the where-abouts and feeding inclination of tench. A cool, clear summer night will send temperatures diving in the shallows so that deeper swims will again be a wise choice for the morning session.

Hot periods in midsummer may, if prolonged, raise temperatures high enough to make tench lethargic. They will feed

Bures Lake on the Suffolk-Essex borders; a haven for great tench of the seventies.

consistently up to about 74° Fahrenheit, beyond which they feed far less until wind or rain or a cooler weather pattern reduces temperature and raises oxygen levels. Night fishing during these periods of the doldrums usually pays off. Tench need less dissolved oxygen than most other species, but even so the weed which gives out oxygen during daytime discharges carbon dioxide at night, which, during heat-waves, may repel tench so that it is better to concentrate on clear water. But these comments only apply to heat-waves. In normal temperatures I have caught enough fish from the middle of weedbeds after dark to know that carbon dioxide bothers anglers more than tench.

BEHAVIOUR

A point I made earlier was that tench in flat-bottomed weedy lakes do not move around much. This makes life easier for the angler; he does not need to worry about intercepting patrollers or locating those hotspot bottom features – though where such features are present they should not be ignored.

A good lake swim will probably always be good unless something alters or destroys it, and I have found that it is possible to catch the same recognisable fish several times over in a short period from the same spot. Since they were never caught else-where I assume that they lived in the swim I caught them from. For this reason a well fished swim may become very hard indeed because its tench become wary.

One swim I recall produced seventeen tench the first time I fished it, so I fished again and again, taking a number of recognisable fish several times over. Then it got more difficult until eventually I was hard pressed to catch even one. In the end I moved just five yards down the bank, dragged a new swim immediately next to the first, and proceeded to catch big bags again – of the same recognisable fish! Lesson: it is not always the bait, the tackle, or the rig which make tench suspicious, but the swim it was caught from.

RAKING

Raking may increase chances on these soft-bottomed waters, but it all depends on the condition of the mud in the chosen swim. Swim beds with clean silt or reasonably firm mud usually respond well, producing mud clouds which linger and continue to attract and keep tench feeding even into the full brightness of day. But bottoms of rotting vegetation or shallows containing black, stinking mud are best left strictly alone. They contain accumulations of toxic gases which, if released, will ruin the swim. The stench of these released gases will not do you any favours either!

The most miserable tench session I ever had was on a lake swim like that. It lay hidden deep in the wooded grounds of a ruined monastery, the gaunt remains of which could still be seen peeping through the vegetation of the far bank. A monk haunted the lake, so they said, the bald-domed apparition rising from the water every second full moon to strike terror into the heart of any unfortunate angler who happened to be abroad at the time. Once my brother Ted and I had heard heavy footfalls approaching us along the over-grown path, and we both swear we saw branches and scrub jostling as something heavy pushed through. But there was no one, nothing, there.

'Monastery pond' always had an omi-nous, eerie atmosphere – always cold and dank around its decaying banks, even on the hottest day. We always fished in pairs, the better to ward off any invasion from

The slacks at the sides of weir pools are reliable places to find river tench.

the phantom monk. But there were good tench to be had and on this particular night session I fished alone. I arrived early in order to rake the swim thoroughly which I thought would really get the tench feeding. A bad mistake – the bottom was of that foul, stinking mud and for hours afterwards the swim bubbled and boiled like a witch's cauldron, filling the air with an almost overpowering stench.

I went through the motions of fishing, with about as much chance of catching a tench out of the ruined swim as a halibut. Soon darkness fell, and with it a deathly quiet fell over the place. No owls, no rats rustled, no small fish flipped – just total silence. And a rising of the hackles on the nape of my neck as though someone, behind me in the gloom, was watching . . .

I spent most of the next hour with my head swivelling like a demented owl, my uneasiness eventually mounting to stark fear. And all the while there was the obnoxious stink as masses of gas bubbles continued to break the surface of the swim. Another fifteen minutes saw me stumbling through the blackness back to the comfort of the van.

No, I did not see the monk – but I am quite certain that he saw me. Perhaps my rake disturbed his watery grave.

Rivers

River tench are simply tench which live in rivers, and all the comments I have made about lakes apply. River tench seem parti-

A slow, deep stretch of the Suffolk Stour at Sudbury; a classical river tench habitat.

cularly attracted to the shade afforded by lilies, even though there may be lots of softer types of weed nearby. I confess that I do not really understand this love of lilies by tench or anglers, for they provide precious little else but cover, which tench could obtain from weed types more beneficial to them. There are probably a few snails and their eggs, and the odd grub or two attached to the underside of the pads, but lilies provide far less food than does soft weed. They do have an aesthetic attraction for us anglers, but the numbers of lost tench they are responsible for negates that advantage.

An old-timer once said that he always fished at the base of lily stems with garden peas as bait, because, he said, they resembled the little green pods of new growth at the base of the stems which tench liked to eat, which was why they were attracted to lilies. I never did see him catch a tench on his green peas, though I often spied him fishing by lilies with lobs, so I remain dubious about those little green pods.

Be that as it may, tench do like lilies, and in rivers and drains, which usually have good beds along the margins, there is no better place to find them.

In stretches of river with neither lilies nor soft weed I have had some success by selecting a reeded margin where there is a reasonable drop-off into deeper water tight up to the reed fringe. The important point is to place the bait tight up to the stems. You could probably entice tench

The patch of lily pads on the right is small, but large enough to conceal several river tench.

further out into open water by groundbait, but since these reed-stem tench invariably bolt *outwards* when they feel the hook, rather than into the stems, I think it is sensible to fish for them where they would rather be instead of where you would prefer to catch them.

Most rivers and drains shelve gradually a short distance from the bank then drop sharply into deeper water. Tench like the shelves, and I have done best by fishing them at an angle along the bank, well away from the spot where I am putting the bait. There is often sparse bank cover, so it pays to keep out of sight and away from the skyline above the swim.

TACKLE, TECHNIQUES AND BAITS

12 · Tackle

One of the great attractions of tench fishing is the wide variety of methods by which they can be caught. Not only that, tench are notorious for changing whims at the drop of a hat, and one can never totally rely on being successful with the same method, swim, or even water for two days running. Being equipped with the right tackle to handle these changes in habits helps to keep the landing net wet.

Watercraft and knowledge of the life-style and feeding habits of tench will in my opinion always be more important than tackle, but a combination of know-how plus good-quality versatile equipment is a hallmark of the consistently successful angler. Having made those points, I shall assume that the reader already has a basic knowledge of tackle requirements and shall therefore discuss only the most important items.

Rods

A fishing rod is a very personal item of tackle indeed, and what suits one may be regarded as useless by another. Therefore, apart from stating that carbon is superior in every way for tench rods, I shall not be specific with brand names, but will deal only with lengths and actions that I find suit me.

FLOAT-FISHING RODS
At one time I owned, and at various times used, about half a dozen different float rods. But the arrival of carbon gave an unexpected bonus: not only does it make better fishing rods, but far more versatile ones too. By that I mean that fewer types of rod are needed to do the same job; one carbon rod will do the same range of work as two or even three of glass fibre.

All my glass rods have been either sold or pensioned off. I now use just three different float rods of carbon fibre. The first and most used is a 13-foot medium-fast action which was originally designed for heavier types of match fishing. This rod, while being progressively powerful through the middle and butt sections, has a tip of fine diameter but snappy action, responsive and ideal for cushioning fast striking with fine tackle, which is generally what I use the rod for. Note that the tip, while being of low diameter, is not a spliced tip. All spliced-tip rods I have seen have been hopeless for tench fishing, being just too sloppy for positive striking and spoiling the feel of the rod in casting and playing fish. My rod is perfect for situations where tench will only accept tiny baits in open water, for example maggots or casters used as loose feed and hook bait, with small hooks on fine hook lengths.

I have discussed the finer details of this method in the next chapter, but for the moment we need a rod capable of dotting the tiny bites usually experienced with this sort of fishing, and that described does the job admirably. I can go as fine as a hook length of 1·7lb BS and a size 20 hook, and have taken tench up to 7lb 6oz on such fine end tackle with no problems, the fine tip

Len Head was obliged to scale down to a 1lb 7oz hooklink and size 18 hook to fool this late season tench of 7lb 6oz.

cushioning the strike and responding perfectly to the sudden lunges of the fighting tench.

I use this rod for heavier work too, in particular longer-range float work using big antennas and sliding-float rigs. The middle sections provide plenty of power for steering fish away from trouble.

The second rod is used for heavy float fishing with big baits in and around weed and snags. Small baits more often than not provoke small bites; big baits, on the other hand, more often produce nice bold bites, particularly when fishing around dense weed. Fast striking is rarely necessary so the most important properties of the rod are that it should be powerful enough to balance the 5 to 7lb BS lines required in such swims, and have an all-through action to avoid tackle breakage and retain the hook-hold during what is usually a close-range tussle.

A longish rod is useful to give good line pick-up on the strike and to hold the line above any emergent weed between rod tip and float. The extra length is also valuable for holding fish as they dive towards marginal weed. Mine is 12 feet in length. Some blanks sold as light Avons are adequate for heavy float work, though most are on the short side at about 11 feet. You can of course glue a short section into the butt to provide the extra length if you are building your own rod, without in any way spoiling the blank's action.

I use the third rod on comparatively rare

occasions, because at 15 feet long, with a moderately powerful medium-fast action, it is quite a handful and not the most pleasant rod in the world to use. I use it for fishing the fringes of wide belts of marginal rushes and for this it is invaluable because, by playing the tench directly under the tip, it is possible to disorientate it during the fight and so prevent it diving into the rushes. The leverage even a moderate-sized tench can exert when hooked directly under the tip of a 15-foot rod has to be experienced to be appreciated. But on this rod they usually come out, which they may not do on a shorter one because of the difficulty in keeping them away from the reed fringe. I have not been able to find a blank of the right length

A modern doppelgänger; ideal for introducing particle baits to the swim at long range.

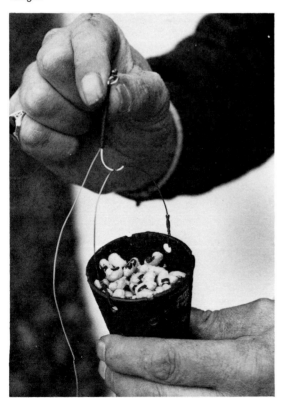

and action in the freshwater range so I adapted mine from a light-action salmon blank.

LEGER RODS

The first priority in any close to medium range leger rod is an easy action. I like to feel the rod through to the handle throbbing and responding to every turn of the fish. At the same time the rod should retain the crispness in action needed for good line pick-up at medium ranges and for pulling home the hook on striking. Since the rod is also required on occasions to flick out soft baits without casting them off the hook, and to lob small swimfeeders to medium ranges, you will appreciate that it needs to be a pretty versatile tool.

If glass fibre was your only choice you would probably have to carry several rods of different tapers to do all these types of fishing, but with the versatility of carbon all you need is just the one. A compound-tapered light Avon of about 1lb test curve and from 11ft to 11ft 6inches long will be found ideal. Several years ago I acquired a pair of 11-foot Avons, into the butts of which I glued a further 6-inch section to provide more versatility and enable them to be used for some float fishing too. They were of progressive yet positive action – perfect in fact – and soon became my favourite rods, still hard at work today. At times I have fished as fine as 3lb BS line and 2lb BS hook lengths, and at others with 8lb line when confronted with densely weeded swims. I can throw a one-ounce lead up to eighty yards and lob a loaded feeder up to sixty.

While rods of the above actions are superb for general close and medium range, and will cope at longer ranges, they lack the power for good hook penetration when striking at long range. A more specialised action is better for swimfeeder fishing at these ranges. A good many years ago, while feeder fishing at Sywell Reservoir, Harry Green and Pete Jackson designed what was, and still is, the ideal action for long-range feeder fishing. Any rod with a stiff tip is liable to empty the feeder with the snatch it produces on the cast, so the rod needs softness in the top third to smooth and cushion the cast. It should, however, be progressively stiffer in the middle section to aid casting and line pick-up, and to pull the hook home.

A rigid butt does nothing for smooth casting so the section just above and under the handle should have some give in it. The perfect feeder rod may be difficult to find but, in the absence of the ideal, stepped-up Avons from 11 to 11½ feet long of 1¼lb test curve will handle most feeder fishing.

LONG-RANGE RODS

Very long casting is rarely necessary in tench fishing, though there will be times or waters when angling pressure or a far-out feature such as a bar or gully may cause tench to be located a long way off. Reaching these fish and striking efficiently at long range was made easier with the early development of fast-tapered glass-fibre rods, and with the arrival of carbon fibre fast tapers are still widely popular. I have never questioned the advantages of fast tapers for long range with glass fibre although I personally took an immediate dislike to their stiff, unfeeling action, and refused to use them even though my prejudice may have cost me a fish or two. I do, however, question the need for fast tapers in carbon-fibre and carbon-composite rods. Carbon, as already mentioned, is far better in both casting and in setting hooks at range than glass ever could be, and a moderately powerful compound

taper in carbon of around 1½lb test curve and up to 13 feet long will cope with all that is required at long range.

You may agree that such a rod would cope, but at the same time argue that the principles of fast tapers are still valid; that they would not only cope but be more efficient for the job. There is no denying the logic of that argument. There is also no denying that there is more to enjoyable tench fishing than numbers in the net. I like to feel the rod with every tench I catch.

Reels

Now and again as a special treat I like to catch tench on a centre-pin reel – not because I catch more but because no other sort of reel gives the same direct feel and contact while playing a tench. Centre-pins are much more enjoyable for close-in swims.

Apart from these occasions, all my tench fishing is done with medium-sized fixed-spool reels. My reels must be robust, reliable, quiet, and fitted with free-turning rollers in the bale arm. I have found none to better my old model Mitchell 300s for virtually all heavy float fishing and for legering. The wide spools and excellent line-lay also make them suitable for long-range work. Mitchell 300s do have a rather unreliable clutch system, which causes line to be yielded in jerks while fish are being played. They also alter tension with variations in temperature, so that a setting which works in the warmth of a summer's day may virtually lock up with the cooling of the air at night. Thus one is continually fiddling with it to

Opposite *The tench cannot slip out of this weigh-sling, and the scales are accurate - important considerations for all good tench men.*

retain the right setting. The drag system is also outdated, the clutch knob setting being at the front of the spool, which makes adjustment whilst playing fish awkward.

These are annoying points to the angler who likes to play fish from the clutch, but since I prefer to backwind the reel to fighting fish these clutch inadequacies do not worry me. I always screw the drag setting knob up tight, fish and strike with the ratchet switch on, but flick it to the off position simultaneously with the strike so that there is no danger of breaking off either on striking or when a tench bolts when it feels the hook.

Modern reel manufacturers seem to have decided that we need silent anti-

Doug Wood places a small intruder into the author's modified keepsack.

reverse ratchets on our reels. Personally, I want a quiet ratchet but one I can hear – there is nothing more annoying than having to keep fiddling about after dark checking whether the ratchet switch is on or off.

However, a flush of excellent fixed-spools is currently appearing on the tackle shelves, many of which have superbly smooth slipping clutches. Although I prefer the better feel of the fish offered by backwinding, I make an exception for fine-tackle float fishing. Backwinding is then not sensitive enough because the slightest unexpected plunge of a tench can snap the fine line before you are able to yield any from the handle. An ultra-smooth slipping clutch responds better for this method and I switch to using a Cardinal 54 or a new graphite Penn model shortly to be marketed here. Both have the drag-setting knob situated at the rear of the reel for easy adjustment.

Lines

The perfect line for general tench fishing needs above all to be reliable, to have consistent diameter, good abrasion resistance and knot strength, and moderate elasticity. I try all new brands as they become available but always return to the tried and tested Maxima, which, I find, provides all the above requirements in addition to being of a sensible dark bronze colour, which blends well with the subdued underwater surroundings in which tench live.

Maxima sinks quickly and is particularly suitable for legering and float-fishing methods requiring a sunk line between rod and float. Other float methods require a brand which floats more readily, and also one that is finer in diameter for its strength

A rod with plenty of action allows 'bouncing' the tench with no fear of breakage.

to aid better tackle control. Trilene, Bayer, and Racine are all good choices.

Some anglers use a pre-stretched line for long-range fishing because it provides a quicker, more positive contact with the fish on striking. Pre-stretched lines have significantly lower diameter for a given breaking strain, with obvious advantages in casting and bait presentation, but have less latitude and so give a lower margin of safety because they are liable to snap under sudden stress. While not denying their usefulness at long range, I have found their resistance to abrasion and therefore their reliability very unsatisfactory, and cannot recommend them. I do, however, find a use for them for short hook lengths in situations where I do not want to scale down the breaking strain of the main line, but want a finer diameter near the hook. In this case the lack of elasticity in the hook length is compensated for by the stretch in the main line, and any fault in the hook length, such as abrasions, is easily spotted.

For long range I stick with Maxima, adding a shock leader of Sylcast – probably the toughest line of all – when really belting a lead out or where the last few yards of line may scrape over gravel bars or sharp-shelled molluscs like zebra mussels.

Hooks

Some of the best tench anglers I know swear by spade-end hooks, but my own preference is for eyed hooks. If you examine the tops of many spade hooks they often feel not sharp but not blunt either, which they would have to be for me to trust them not to cut through the line under tension. In fact I do know of cases of this happening. A valid point raised by Pete Jackson is that sometimes the hook penetrates through to the hilt and the point takes a second hold outside the mouth. When this happens extracting the hook causes less damage if it is pulled right through the outside and the line is cut above it. Pete maintains that a spade-end is easier to pull through and indeed he is right, so they are worth consideration.

As to pattern, every angler has his own preference. I like a bronzed medium-length shank, with a straight but slightly offset point. An offset point retains a better hook-hold than a straight one, an important consideration when you have tench charging about in weedbeds.

I prefer a micro-barb. When I use a hook with too large a barb I nip it in with forceps to leave just a bump. I do not use totally barbless hooks. All hooks need sharpening and checking for faults in temper and non-closure of the eye, though it is rare to find a faulty hook in the Partridge specialist range which I use for most tench fishing. Kamatsu and Drennen chemically sharpened hooks are also excellent and unbelievably sharp, and the Drennen Super Specialist range are the strongest hooks I have ever seen and ideal for fishing in weed jungles.

Accessories

KEEPNETS AND KEEPSACKS

Years ago, Harry Green modified his keepnet to incorporate a lining, or internal sleeve of loose-weave hessian sacks, and found that tench lay quieter inside them. Tench which stay quiet in nets lose less protective slime, and his idea was a vast improvement on conventional keepnets. Even micromesh nets cause damage, and unless they are modified in a similar manner they are, as far as I am concerned, obsolete.

Carp anglers have given us the industrial nylon keepsack, far superior for retaining all sorts of fish, including tench, since they cause the absolute minimum of stress and no damage at all, providing they are not overcrowded. Tench stay quiet in the sacks for the same reason they did in Harry's net – because it is dark. Keepsacks roll into a small package so it is convenient to carry two or three to distribute a large catch. They dry quicker, are less smelly, are lighter, and have everything to commend them over nets.

I have modified my own tench sacks by inserting a rigid ring through the hem at the top. The rings are fitted with a standard bank stick thread so that I am able to use them open-topped exactly as I would a keepnet.

LANDING NETS

I believe that a round frame is preferable to a triangular one for netting tench because the fish can be brought over it from any angle without loss of frame diameter; if you bring a tench to the side of a triangular net it is presented with the narrowing part of the triangle. I use a 24-inch folding round frame with a 30-inch-deep soft knitted mesh. Normal folding round frames are too weak and I am currently looking at the more robust salmon versions.

FLOAT PATTERNS

A look into my float box betrays me as one of those compulsive collectors. There are

The Dacron hooklink is clearly visible with this beaten tench.

short fat ones, long thin ones, cork-bodied floats and floats of balsa. There are transparent floats, camouflaged floats, floats with sight bobs and floats without, bodied floats and straight floats, floats with tips of every hue and colour. Most of them I have never used and probably never will.

Realistically, two or three basic patterns in different sizes are all that is needed for 95 per cent of float fishing. My most-used are antennas with slim onion-shaped balsa bodies in sizes from 1 BB up to 3 swan shot. For general medium-range fishing I find a low-buoyancy antenna of cane to be most sensitive, though my box also contains some with peacock quill or sarkandas reed antennas for choppy water conditions, for long-range float fishing, and whenever more stability is required, such as in countering a strong undertow.

Straight reversed peacock quills (the thin end at the top) are superb tench-fishing floats, extremely buoyant and taking a good shot loading yet very sensitive indeed, ideal for fishing the lift, laying on, float legering or drift methods described later. I carry odd lengths of quill and cut bits off when I need them.

A pattern useful for windy conditions when waves obscure ordinary antennas is the Drennen Driftbeater, an antenna float with a sight bob on the tip. The thin antenna retains sensitivity but the float remains visible and the buoyant bob aids stability.

The only other pattern I use regularly is a bodied peacock antenna with a finer-diameter short cane tip insert. This float, shotted to within a quarter of an inch of the tip, is ultrasensitive for those times when tench are particularly cautious and tiny baits and bites are the only option.

LEGER INDICATORS

It is said that the most sensitive leger bite indicator is the bow of line at the rod tip, and in calm water it is indeed a good method. Better still in my view is a small dough bobbin nipped on the line just in front of the rod tip – every bit as sensitive yet far more visible. The rod is set in the rests horizontal with the bank and the soft ball of paste arranged to hang so that it sits just above water level. Providing it is soft it flies off the line when you strike.

Good though the above methods are, you need to wade to the rod tip to replace the indicator after each cast, or sit well back from the margin so that you can reach the tip from the bank. Neither is always practical, and many good tench fishers prefer the convenience of a swing-tip. Personally I hate them hanging about on the ends of my rods. They seem cumbersome and certainly spoil the feel of the rod and the fish. For those reasons I never use them, but acknowledge their value as a tip indicator. Longer swingtips up to about 18 inches will be found better for tench fishing than short ones.

Quivertips for tench are not as daft as they might seem and I often use one for shy biters. A half-inch twitch from a shy tench on a butt indicator takes some hitting, but on a quivertip the same twitch is registered more deliberately – the tip holds for just that split second longer to enable a strike. Set the rod at an angle along the bank, with the tip low to the water. The above indicators all work well, as do many other simple butt indicators, such as washing up liquid bottle tops, or silver paper tubes, and so on.

I have noticed that many tench anglers habitually use monkey climbers on needles, apparently regardless of the bait or method in use at the time. The idea of monkey climbers was first devised for carp fishing by Rick Gibbinson. The idea was brilliant and at times it works as well for tench as it does for carp. Those times are when tench are boldly taking boilies or when a bolt rig is used (of which more later) or whenever resistance at the indicator end is not an important factor. But you have only to conduct a simple experiment to discover that at other times and for more conventional methods monkey climbers offer far too much resistance. Simply add shot to the line above the monkeys, and then above a light butt indicator, and note the difference.

Now and again I do use monkey climbers, usually to counteract strong winds, having made my own from 1-inch diameter polystyrene balls. Used with thin polished stainless-steel needles they are reasonably sensitive. But to use them always, regardless, will cost you tench.

AN IMPROVED INDICATOR

I am never happy using any type of indicator which involves fiddling about clipping it to the line or resetting it after every cast. On far too many occasions a bite comes whilst putting them in position, usually resulting in a missed chance because you are not ready.

The perfect indicator needs to be easily visible, quick to set into position, and light but adjustable with extra weight when required. For a good many years I used a simple small plastic ring between butt and second ring, a method which still works well. However, over a period of time the ring has been modified (see page 127) and now incorporates a 300-microlambert

Opposite   A round frame, 24-inch diameter landing net is perfect for tench fishing.

betalight and a clip whipped to the rod above the butt ring, in which the indicator is housed during casting or whenever it is not required for use.

After casting it is simply flipped out of the clip, dropping immediately into the V fishing position with absolutely no delay. And there is no more fiddling about whilst twitching the bait back, because after pulling in a little line the indicator drops back into position by itself. Tench are played with the indicator still on the line. Extra weight to counteract undertow is added in the form of a coil of thin lead wire, and the indicator can be stabilised by using a needle in windy conditions.

Electronic indicators, of which Optonics are certainly the best, are an essential part of many forms of legering. They allow you to take your eyes off the indicators and so be on the lookout for signs of fish, perhaps a patch of bubbles or a tench rolling quietly over in the surface, which you would almost certainly miss if you were obliged to sit with your head down staring at the indicators in order to see a bite.

Minor Accessories

What about the sundry bits and pieces found in a tench fisher's rucksack, which individually perhaps do not appear significant but together do play an important role in the properly equipped angler's armoury?

Speaking of rucksacks, I can heartily recommend one to any angler who still lumbers to the lake loaded down with boxes, baskets, buckets, etc., swinging about. Rucksacks swallow up all your equipment, including chair, rod rests, spare clothing, food, etc., so that it is all carried on your back as one unit, leaving your hands free to look after the rods. Make sure you acquire a waistband with a rucksack, which buckles tightly around your waist and distributes the weight upon your hips as well as shoulders. Rods are made up before a session, the sections broken down, secured with elastic bands top and bottom, and parcelled together with landing-net handle and brolly with two velcro straps. I never use rod holdalls, though one or two modern versions which take ready-made-up rods, including reels, are certainly worth consideration.

As well as equipment already discussed, a rummage in my own rucksack reveals Avon scales to 32lb, the adjustment wheel tightened with felt washers to decrease the tendency for them to bounce off the correct setting, together with a home-made nylon banana-shaped weigh-bag. Two catapults, one for balls of ground-bait, another for loose feed. A tub of 'putty' made from fuller's earth and gly-cerine which, rubbed on the line, sinks it. Another tub, with Mucilin to float the line. A tin of vaseline, which I smear on any wounds found on a tench. A selection of swimfeeders. A box containing spools of Dacron of 3lb and 6lb BS for hook links, and 1lb BS for hair rigs. Old hinged tobacco boxes containing my hooks. Plastic bags containing PVA water-soluble string and tape. A bait dropper which I never use. A tin with spare indicators, batteries, bale arm springs, line clips, and adhesive tape for repairs. Plus a tupper-ware partitioned box containing the multitude of other bits and pieces an angler uses – shot, leads, beads, swivels and line stops. Compass, thermometer, scissors, forceps, hook sharpeners, superglue brolly pegs and a few dozen other small items complete this rather short list of tench fishers' requirements.

13 · Float Fishing

A cork float with crimson tip is very necessary to proper angling for tench.

I have never read anything that quite captured the essence of drowsy summer days spent float fishing for tench like the chapter on 'A Brace of Tench' in Hugh Sheringham's book *An Angler's Hours,* published in 1905.

A cork float with crimson tip is very necessary to proper angling for tench; it supplies the one touch of colour that is wanting in the landscape, and it is a satisfying thing to look upon. A severely practical mind might argue that it is as visible to the fish as to the fisherman, and might suggest a fragment of porcupine quill as being less ostentatious. But, however one regards it, tench fishing is a lengthy occupation, and must be approached with a leisurely mind. The sordid yearning for bites must not be put in the balance against artistic effect. Besides, it may be said of tench more emphatically than of most other fish; if they are going to feed they are, and if they are not they most certainly are not. As a rule they are not, and their feelings are therefore not so important as the angler's.

Traditional Float Rigs

Several traditional methods have stood the test of time and are as good as ever today, providing some forethought is put into their use. Sheringham's angler using the cork float with crimson tip employed perhaps the oldest method of all – laying on. Modern tench men may be tempted to pooh-pooh the idea, but I still use it often. It comes into its own with big baits, in small clearings in overgrown swims, or when tench seem to want lots of time to take the bait properly.

The old way was to place all the shot some distance from the hook and set the float slightly overdepth so that all the shot lay on the bottom. This leads to dropped baits when the tench feel the lead, so I modify my laying-on rig as shown in Fig 1. Set the float – I like a peacock or porcupine quill – about 18 inches deeper than the swim, nip enough shot on the line to just cock it, then slide the bottom shot, preferably a number 1 or BB, down the line so that it alone rests on the bottom. The float will now lie at half-cock and either falls flat or glides along the surface, sub-merging slowly, when a tench takes. Real Mr Crabtree stuff.

Another effective but neglected method is float legering, but I cannot recall when I last saw a tench angler using it. One of the biggest bags I ever had came to float-leger tactics, close to 100lb of tench on a day when I failed to catch by any other method I was equipped at the time to use. I had started off legering, but, with no bites, I began to believe no tench were there until

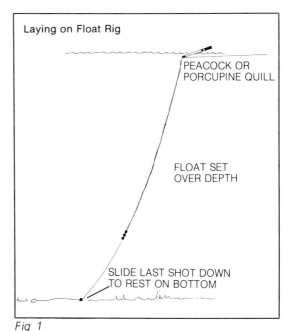

Fig 1

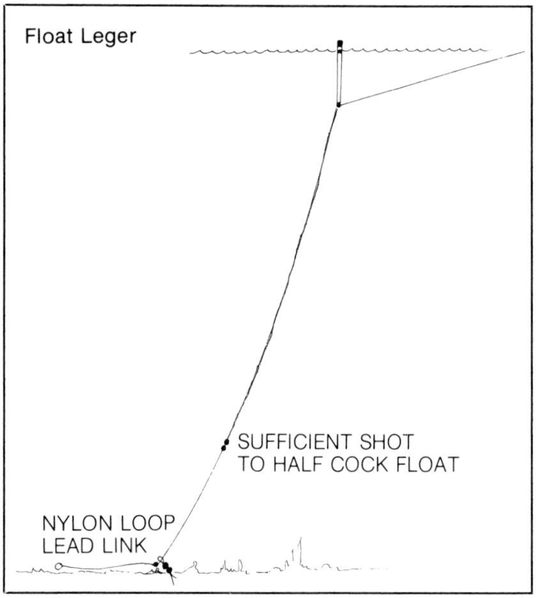

Fig 2

I accidentally hooked one when I wound in to rebait. So I concentrated harder, watching the line at the rod tip where it dimpled into the calm water. After a while it twitched a quarter of an inch, no more, and my strike on the only rod I had with me, a slow-action 11-footer, was a mile too late.

Several missed twitches later I changed to as delicate a float rig as I could manage on the inappropriate tackle. That resulted in minute dips of the float tip which the soft rod was again unable to cope with. I then set up a float leger using a 4-inch length of peacock quill set well overdepth, with a sliding lead stopped just two inches from the hook. After casting all was tightened to the lead until a speck of float tip was visible. Those unhittable tweaks turned into positive indications, the float disappearing promptly, and I hardly missed another bite.

But tench do not have to be twitchers for the float leger to be useful. You can use it with a longer hook length for slower-biting fish. It can be put to good use for longer range even with small floats, and is particularly valuable to know about when fishing very irregular bottoms, since the overdepth setting still fishes the bait properly.

With a large buoyant-tipped float the method is also handy to prevent the tackle being dragged out of position by strong undertows. Should the float still drag under, fine adjustment can be made to the amount of visible tip by allowing a little free line off the reel spool.

The float leger is usually described as simply stopping a lead the required distance from the hook, no shot being added to cock the float. That way is wrong, because without shotting a fish pulls against the full buoyancy of the float. I always shot up to half-cock, leaving some buoyancy for fine adjustment as described.

The Lift Rig

This rig, developed by Fred J. Taylor, is excellent when tench are inclined to be finicky. Fred lays no claim to its invention.

Accomplished tench catcher Janet Jackson returns a big tench to its home in the Centre Lagoon gravel pit.

Indeed, the method is described in several old angling books as the 'shot leger', but it was he who adapted and developed it and popularised it for tench fishing. Most anglers fishing the lift select a float, add enough shot to cock it, then fish at dead depth with the shot on the bottom, which is not the way Fred originally devised it. The correct way is to select the shot size first, anything from a single BB to a swan depending upon the range, and then snip sections off a piece of peacock quill until the shot sinks it slowly. The float is fixed bottom end only and set slightly deeper than the depth of the swim, the rod is placed in rests and the line tightened until the float cocks. When a tench picks up the bait it dislodges the shot too, so the float falls flat. A strike at that precise moment nearly always results in a hooked fish; too late and the tench will probably have already rejected the bait.

Fred stressed the importance of leaving the rod untouched in the rests until the float keels over, and of tuning your striking arm finely in order to hit bites quickly. The lift works particularly well with buoyant crust, with the anchor shot set one or two inches away, and in my experience it works best with biggish baits. Tiny baits generally call for a very small anchor shot and float, and fishing range, weather conditions, and so on, can make that very difficult except at close range.

Fishing buoyant crust with an almost vertical line to the float does mean that the bait floats up immediately parallel with the line just above the shot, leading to many false bites from tail wash as tench move about near the tackle. You are liable to find yourself swatting away at these registrations and often foul-hooking a fish as the hook catches a fin. I find it better to set the float well overdepth, giving a lower angle of line to the shot. That lessens but

does not totally remedy the problem. Now and again the float will go under instead of falling flat, but it does not matter whether it comes up or goes down – either way you strike instantly.

The three rigs so far described are fine when tench will accept a firmly anchored sizeable bait, but occasions arise often enough when they will have nothing to do with them, especially after the June feeding spree is over, when they become more wary and difficult to tempt. Even on those days when you have caught a few fish on biggish baits bites are likely to tail off towards the end of the feeding spell, and then small baits can add a few more fish to the bag. They generally work better towards the end of the season too. And even when large baits might have proved effective anglers tend to force tench into preoccupied feeding on tiny items by heavy groundbaiting with such baits as maggots and casters.

Antenna Rigs

Tiny baits demand more sensitive float rigs. We have match anglers to thank for

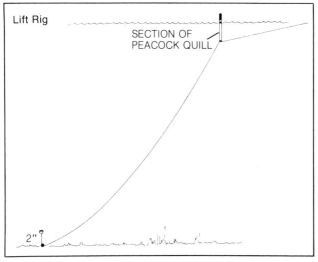

Lift Rig

SECTION OF PEACOCK QUILL

2"

Fig 3

A vast assortment of floats, yet just a few patterns are adequate for nearly all tench fishing.

such advances in modern float design as antennas, which are perfect for these finer aspects of float fishing. Fig 4 shows the rig I like for shy feeders on small baits. The exact placing of the bulk shot is a matter of your own preference. I group them as shown, but match men usually prefer to use them as locking shot either side of the float ring. Doing so means that the float precedes the bait on casting and the line needs to be feathered by the application of slight friction as it leaves the reel, which slows the flight so that the tackle straightens just before it alights. I prefer the end tackle to precede the float. Neither way will affect sensitivity unless you happen to be looking for bites on the drop, which is not often in tench fishing.

What does affect sensitivity is the diameter of the bit of float protruding above the surface. A thin antenna at the tip is obviously more sensitive than a thick one, though except for very close-range work 2mm is the thinnest I can comfortably see. At longer range it becomes necessary to use a thicker one or preferably stick to a thin one with a sight bob. Antenna floats come in all sorts of shapes, sizes and materials, loaded and unloaded, with and without finer tip inserts or sight bobs. For the majority of swims I like a balsa or cork body with a 2mm diameter straight cane antenna. Cane is not very buoyant, allowing plenty of lift movement from the number 1 shot I use as a trigger.

Weather conditions and the distance fished affect the choice of float on the day.

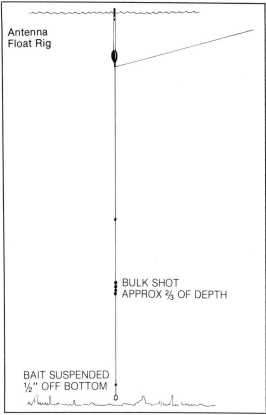

Fig 4

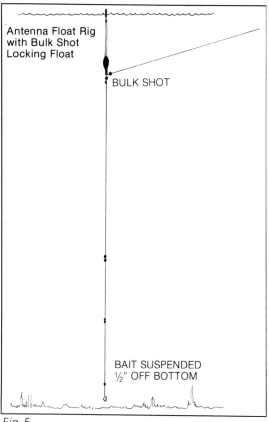

Fig 5

A chop on the surface calls for more buoyant, thicker stems of peacock or sarkandas, and longer floats aid submersion of the line below surface drag. In heavy surface flows a small shot can be nipped on about eighteen inches above the float, which sinks the line deeper still. However, big floats, choppy swims, and thick antennas defeat the object of extreme sensitivity to register tiny bites, so it may be better to look at other methods.

Plumbing the swim accurately is vital when fishing the rig shown, for the float is set to suspend the bait half an inch off bottom. That precise setting is important for two reasons: first, tench take the suspended bait more readily than one on the bottom when feeding on small items, which swirl up from the bottom with the activity in the swim; second, it is quite impossible for a tench to take the suspended bait without registering a bite, which can happen with a bottom-fished bait.

The indication from a finicky tench is a small but deliberate dip of the float tip, probably not submerging even a quarter of an inch. But that's it, and you must be prepared to dot it quickly. I always fish with the rod at an angle to the float, the middle supported by a rest and holding the butt, which is resting on a knee. That way and I am ready to respond the instant the float moves. Delay and you miss it because it is not often these wary fish tow the float right under.

Despite my comments about suspending the bait, there are times when one anchored to the bottom does score better. Try sliding the float up an inch or two and moving a shot down so that it sits on the bottom. Adjust the hook length as necessary – longer for better bites, shorter for tweaks. Lift bites are normal with this alternative rig, though once again all you may get is a tiny movement if tench are in that kind of feeding mood.

These antenna rigs require intense concentration, but both are deadly for shy feeders. Waters where they really come into their own are those with little weed growth where it is feasible to scale down to really fine tackle. I never hesitate to fine down to very fine hook lengths when appropriate, though it is irresponsible to

even consider these tactics in weedy waters; they would certainly result in the poor old tench swimming about trailing broken end tackle.

Sliders

At ranges up to about thirty-five yards sliding floats can give the edge over legering by earlier and better bite indication as well as superior bait presentation. Weather conditions are again the deciding factor. Big waves and undertows make any float method impractical at long range.

Part-loaded antennas such as missiles and zoomers are favoured by match anglers but remember that they are looking for bites on the drop and do not want lots of lead below the float. Nine times out of ten I want the bait to get down quickly and

A light Avon carbon rod - perfect for general tenching.

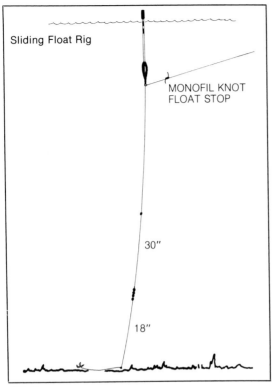

Sliding Float Rig

MONOFIL KNOT
FLOAT STOP

30"

18"

Fig 6

stick doggedly to unloaded patterns. Sliding rigs are notoriously prone to tangling but by using the shotting pattern as shown in Fig 6, and checking the line before the tackle alights, tangling is minimised. Never undergun yourself with too small a sliding float, as striving for distance with insufficient weight leads to inaccurate and erratic casting as well as to tangles. Use one with a large enough shot loading to overcast the fishing spot, then thrust the rod tip underwater to sink the line while retrieving the tackle back into position.

Accurate depth setting again pays off. For big baits the bottom shot should just sit on the bottom and be big enough to submerge the antenna to within about an inch of the tip. Length of tail from shot to hook depends on the sort of bites you get, up to 18 inches for good ones, an inch or two for twitchers. As a rule bites are registered

by the antenna lifting like a marine's sub periscope, but of course the amount of lift is controlled by the size of the trigger shot together with the material and diameter of the antenna.

If there is any undertow the trigger shot needs to be biggish, at least a BB, because a smaller one allows the tackle to be dragged out of position. Good floats to counter undertows are those with sight bobs, because the added tip buoyancy helps prevent the float dragging under against the inertia of the anchored shot.

Preloaded Floats

One of the finest exponents of float fishing for tench I have ever seen is a former

The sun is up, it is midday, but Pete knows tench feed at odd times and remains watchful.

Tenchfishers colleague, Les Millington, who adapts his antenna floats so that they all carry the same amount of shot. He does this by wrapping lead wire around the base, and Les preloads and tests them in his bath so that an equivalent of about two BB added to the line below the loaded float cocks them with the same amount of tip showing.

The advantages are obvious. By using a quick release float attachment it is a simple matter to change to a larger or smaller version to suit varying conditions during a session, without having to alter the shot loading down the line.

A Stand-by Rig

A little-used but excellent rig for fishing deep swims at longer range without resorting to sliders or legering is illustrated in Fig 7. An even more useful advantage is that the line from rod tip to float is deeply sunk, thus curing the problem of surface drift. In use it looks a little silly, the float dangling down alongside the shot, but do not let that bother you – it is tench in the net that counts. The important point to remember is that the distance from A to B should be about a third of that from B to C, otherwise the rig is prone to tangles.

A Simple Set-up

There is nothing at all fancy about this rig, which I devised for big baits and bold bites, but it is one of the best when used at the right times and in the right swims. The float, a small piece of peacock quill, is set to fish the bait at dead depth and is cocked by the weight of the bait alone – no lead. Large baits are necessary to give cocking

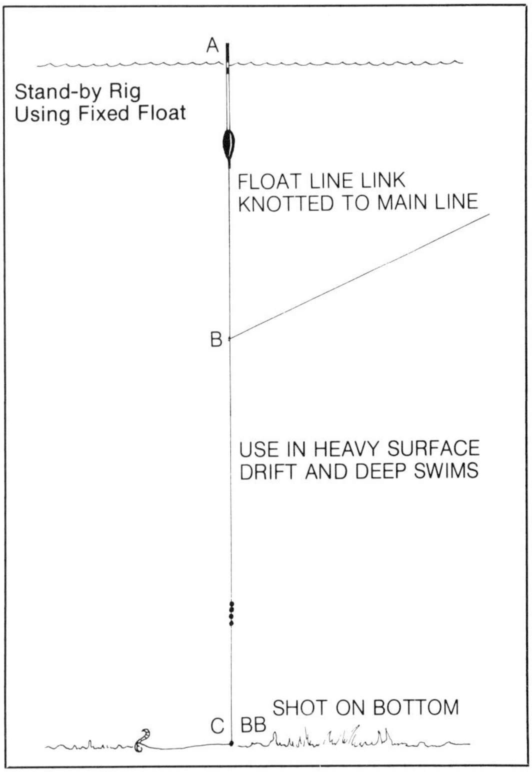

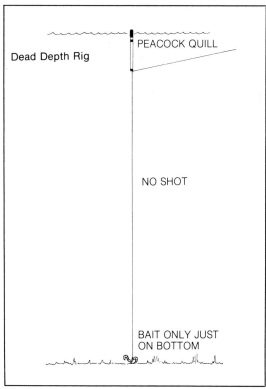

Fig 7

Fig 8

weight, such as big wodges of flake, lobworm, or mussel. Fishing a lively lob on the rig is fascinating; the float fidgets about on the surface as the worm levers itself against the bottom. The rig is good in the early season before tench have had a hammering and when they will still take sizeable baits. But it also works in over-grown swims where security gives them the confidence to accept big mouthfuls. Tench usually retire into the edges of weedbeds when the main feeding spell is over or when light intensity becomes too strong, though they may well continue to feed there.

A bait placed accurately at the very edge of the weed then stands a good chance of being taken. Accuracy is the word – a few feet short will not do. Ordinary float tackle cannot cope, because even though the cast is accurate the bait will sink in an arc away from the fringe, settling well short. A large bait on my simple rig sinks vertically where it alights, towing the tiny float along the surface towards the weed as it does so.

Years ago Fred J. Taylor described a rig he and his brothers devised for perch fishing tight to the stems of reed beds. The float, again peacock, was fixed with double rubbers capping both ends so that there were no protruding bits to snag up. It was also self-cocking so that it preceded the bait when cast, whereupon the bait sank in an arc towards the rushes. I do not know if Fred ever used it for weedbed tench, but I have and it works perfectly.

A tightly shotted slider rig does the same job, but not quite so well. Using my rig, and Fred's too if it is fished dead depth, results in lots of float tip movement when tench are about. It creeps along, dips or rises a little, waggles about, and generally will not sit still. But that is not a deterrent

to the method. In fact I love to see these visible signs of tench stirring below, and in any case a bite is always obvious – the float either lifts and topples or gives a deliberate bob before sliding away and under. Finicky bites are rare on this rig, the tench feeling virtually no resistance.

Dobbing

My friend Arthur Russell uses a float method not dissimilar: no shot, small float, and a big heavy bait – in his case paste. The main difference is that he sets the float slightly deeper than the swim so it lies flat until line is tightened against the big bait to half cock it. Russ uses it in swims where others fear to tread, even the tiniest weed holes. He just plops the bait in the hole – whereupon its weight gets it to the bottom – tightens, puts the rod in the rests, and waits for a tench browsing below the weed to find it. He uses it when tench have (supposedly) stopped feeding well into the day, and continues catching when others have left for home. Weed-hole tench do not mess about with the bait, and the rod is likely to go with it if you do not watch out.

Drifting Rig

There are days when moving baits are taken while stationary ones are ignored. These occasions often but not always coincide with an undertow along the bottom, when I presume tench are feeding on food items washed along with the current. However, I have known dragged baits to do well when there has been no undertow, so that is not the whole answer.

Undertows can be strong enough to trot a bait much as you would in a river – in fact the rig shown in Fig 9 is one I frequently use in rivers. The float, with antenna of

An onion float with slim cane antenna is one of the most useful tench patterns.

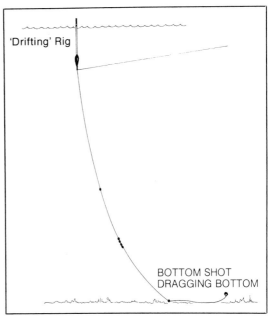

'Drifting' Rig

BOTTOM SHOT
DRAGGING BOTTOM

Fig 9

quill or sarkandas, is slightly undershotted to allow a good inch of visible tip, and set about 18 to 24 inches deeper than the swim. The bottom shot is placed so that it drags bottom, slowing the progress of the bait. In use the bottom shot continually catches on debris so that the float begins to drag under, but its tip buoyancy pops the shot clear again and the tackle continues its erratic course, dipping and lifting through the swim.

Bites are shown by the float lifting more deliberately, or more often by a positive dip followed by a slow sail-away as the tench sucks in the bait and moves off. A semi-buoyant bait which drifts along just off bottom helps progress and presentation, and wind itself can be utilised to produce a dragging bait, perhaps with greater effect, because tench will not necessarily be found where undertows are really strong.

14 · Legering

Freelining

The most resistance-free leger rig ever is freelining, that is, using no lead at all, with only the weight of the bait for casting, and with bites shown by a small indicator near the butt ring, or the bow of line at the rod tip. I rarely use the method because I have known far too many occasions when the fish moved sideways with the bait, failing to register the bite in any way.

I came unstuck like that many times at Manea Pit, freelining with mussels. I would fish along channels fringed either side with walls of Norfolk reed, placing the bait at the base of the stems to one side. Come dawn with no bites it was not uncommon to wind in and find the bait twenty yards across the channel alongside the opposite reed wall, where a tench had taken it then spat it out. After about a dozen lost chances I changed rigs – I am quick to learn!

A Variation on Freelining

When I do freeline it is for presentation other than a resistance-free one. The idea is to use a big bait together with a heavy indicator placed between butt and second rod rings. Having cast, tighten gently so that the indicator is pulled up nearly tight to the rod. The weight of the indicator now slowly drags the bait along the bottom as it falls back to the V position below the rod. A little experiment is needed to get the indicator and bait

The Optonic bite indicator, with Delkim Developments conversion.

balanced just right so that the bait is dragged back very slowly, and the process repeated until a recast is necessary. A deadly method indeed on its day.

Standard Leger Rig

Fig 10 shows the conventional leger rig still popular for close to medium range fishing on a firm bottom. The hook length is variable, depending upon the mood of the

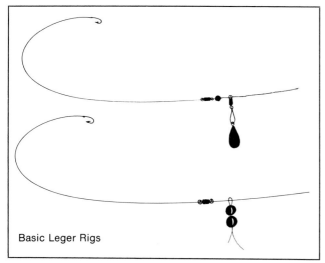

Basic Leger Rigs

Fig 10

tench. Many standardise their hook length at about 18 inches, which is fine for confidently feeding tench, but of no use at all when they are touchy. Then, a longer tail of at least 36 inches and up to 5 feet or even more will produce better pulls. With the short tail, a tench feels resistance upon or immediately after taking the bait, causing it to eject. The longer tail allows more freedom of movement before resistance is felt, by which time the tench is moving away and you get a nice confident take.

This principle applies throughout the range of rigs described in this chapter, with some exceptions, such as when using the bolt or hair rig, of which more later.

One other exception is when you have tench feeding heavily on particles, such as maggots or casters, seed baits, etc. The use of a long tail then can lead to deeply hooked fish, since they will be feeding by sucking in an item then moving only an inch or so before picking up the next. By the time the fish has moved enough to register a bite the hook may easily have already been swallowed – and we must avoid damage to tench at any cost.

When fishing among weed the bomb can be replaced with a loop of line folded over above the leger stop, with swan shot as required nipped onto the ends to form a nylon sliding leger. When a tench hits weed the leger is liable to snag too, and the advantage of the nylon link is that the shot is easily pulled off, giving a direct pull to the tench. It will not cast as well or as accurately as a bomb, and is therefore most useful at short range.

Link Leger

The conventional rig is fine for fishing on a firm bottom, but where the bottom is of soft silt or debris the lead will sink into it, ruining its free-running properties. A link leger (or running paternoster, as some prefer to call it) is then a better choice because the link allows the lead to bury itself while the swivel through which the line runs remains on top of the mud. The length of the link is varied to suit the depth of the silt in the swim; one may require a few inches, while another swim, with a deep layer of liquid mud, will need a much longer link. I have fished lakes with over a foot of liquid mud on the bottom, where leads and baits just disappeared beneath it, making long links and semi-buoyant baits essential. The length of silicone rubber slid over the link as shown in Fig 11 stiffens it and gives tangle-free fishing. At one time I insisted on dull-coloured tubing, browns or blacks, because I feared that brighter colours might put fish off. Then one day I used a length of bright yellow because that was all I had with me, caught a whole bunch of tench, and now do not worry about colour. Tench are curious by nature, investigating anything unusual. Perhaps, like the bunches of brightly coloured flowers in a bottle recommended as attractors by old-time anglers, the coloured tubing, or beads, or whatever, might actually increase catches.

Something I am more fussy about is the incorporation of a small piece of buoyant material like cork or balsa pushed on to the swivel to keep that important bit through which the line runs clear and clean of debris. However, it is a mistake to use so large a piece that the link stands bolt upright on the bottom. When I first used

this buoyancy device I could not figure out why I got lots of half takes, the tench dropping the bait after taking a few inches of line. It was not until I pretended I was a tench by pulling on the bait in clear water that the reason emerged. What happens is that as the bait is given a pull the upright link is pulled over towards it, see-saw fashion. The tench sees this unexpected movement as a threat and drops the bait.

So I reduced the amount of the buoyant material until the link was only slightly more than neutral and sat on the bottom at only a slight angle. It still see-saws to a take, but much less so, and I no longer experience problems with dropped takes.

Leger Stops

These have always been a problem. They either weaken the line or slip in the cast or on the strike. Anyone who uses shot as a stop is asking for trouble. Small pieces of rubber tubing with the line looped through it two or three times are better, but the tube inevitably gets cut through in due course, especially with lower breaking

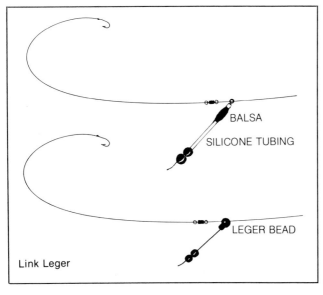

BALSA

SILICONE TUBING

LEGER BEAD

Link Leger

Fig 11

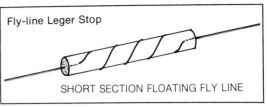

Fly-line Leger Stop

SHORT SECTION FLOATING FLY LINE

Fig 12

The author's indicator and rod clip system - perfect for legering. The cross strut incorporates a betalight.

strain lines, and if that happens with a tench on the end the hook can be bumped clean out of its mouth by the lead falling down the tight line. Plastic plug-in type stops need to be plugged really tightly to prevent them slipping, and a suspicious-looking flat spot is nipped into the line which, although not seriously weakening it, is still less than perfect.

A better idea is to clove-hitch a small piece of tough rubber onto the line. Silicone is no good, it cuts too easily, but the rubber sleeve on high-power electrical flex is OK. Another reasonably reliable stop is a short length of biro tubing, plugged with a tapered match or cocktail stick. If it still slips, two separate stops butted up together will cure the problem.

During a particularly bad spell of breakages at the line stop years ago I began using a short piece of fly line and still swear by it for short-range work. For heavy casting something more robust is needed for the line tends to kink just above a fly-line stop. A section from the middle part of an old fly line is best, being thicker and, if it is from a floater, also slightly buoyant – a small but potentially important point.

The reel line is threaded through the eye of a needle, which is then pushed into the core of the fly-line section at one end and out through the side, wound round three times, then through the side and out through the core the other end. It sounds very fiddly, I know, but Fig 12 explains better and you soon get used to it. The stop is small and neat, will not slip, and does not weaken the line in any measurable way. Tie a hook to the line using any knot you like then pull to breaking-point. You will find it never breaks at the bit of fly line.

The Fixed Paternoster

My experiences with the see-sawing of buoyant running leger rigs started me thinking about just how free a 'free-running' leger really is, for obviously it was line friction at the point where it passed through the leger swivel that caused the problem. I am now convinced that most running leger rigs, most of the time, fail to run at all.

Providing the tench takes line in a straight pull away from the angler, the

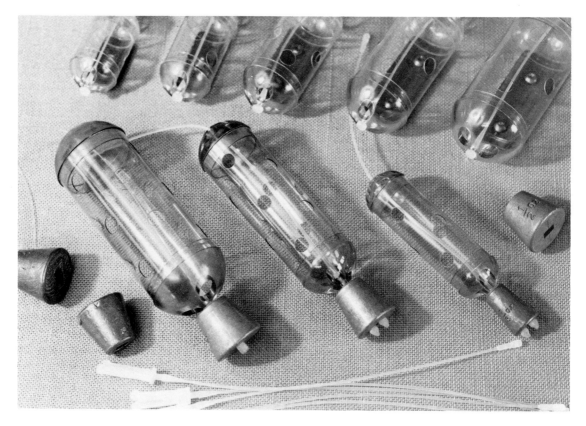

Updated Drennen feeders with their unique system of clip-on interchangeable weights and variable length nylon links.

system works reasonably well, but more often than not it moves off sideways, causing an angle of line at the anchored lead, where friction may be enough to cause the lead to be dislodged. The problem is aggravated at longer range and when using light leger weights, which of course anglers are conditioned to do – how often have you heard the advice to use the minimum amount of lead necessary for the distance fished?

If the tench does not drop the bait on feeling the lead, what now happens is that as it moves off the lead bumps round in fits and starts. Each time it shifts, a little slack line is created which runs through the swivel eye until the angle again causes friction – which shifts the lead again – and so on. If you pick up the rod you can usually feel the bump, pause, bump of this staccato movement. Leave it in the rests and the bite registered is one of those hesitant, jerky affairs which do not seem to develop properly, yet when you strike the tench is yards from where you placed the bait.

Heavy leads go a long way to sorting out the problem, because they stay put against friction. But even so, the longer the fishing range the more pronounced the friction will be, and undertows, etc., can mean that even a heavy lead may shift when a tench takes. Short of getting very wet I cannot prove that happens, but I remain suspicious and now only use a running rig at close range, and then with an oversized lead.

1   *Early summer, and the tranquil surroundings of a lovely tench
lake.*

2　A good angler is always careful about returning tench.

3　An ounce short of the magic seven pounds – but who cares?

4   *Barry Waldon looking pleased with his catch.*

5 *A backcloth of high trees increases the feeding periods of tench.*

6 Arthur Russell is no stranger to big tench; here he returns a chunky Irish fish.

7 The golden tench; perhaps the most handsome of all freshwater fish.

8 Keepsacks retain tench in mint condition.

9 An idyllic lake and a fish on - what more could an angler ask?

10 There are few anglers who do not,
    at some time during summer, fish for
    lovely tench like this.

11 Doug Wood returns the results of a
    morning session.

12   *The sun dips below the trees at Bures Lake.*

These suspicions led me to experiment with fixed paternoster rigs for anything over about twenty yards fishing range, and I soon came to the conclusion that, with limitations, it is far superior to a running rig. The absence of swivels, etc., at the business end means that a taking tench gives a more direct pull to the indicator, bites are generally more confident, and a twitch bite which moves the indicator an inch with a running rig will move it twice as much on a paternoster, often making the difference between a hit or a miss.

Having tried all ways of fixing the paternoster link, such as tying in swivels or moulded metal rings, I now use only the two shown below for close range. Both methods give an unknotted line straight through to the hook, which is an advantage over the three knots necessary with rings and swivels. However carefully you tie knots, a failure is more likely with three than one.

As I said, there are limitations. With, say, a 15-inch paternoster link the tench can only take that length of line before it comes up against the lead. So set the bite indicator to allow that same maximum of lift – that is, a 15-inch drop below the rod if using a butt indicator – and strike before it reaches its limit. That way you hit the fish before it feels the lead. I use a shorter drop anyway, and strike as soon as the indicator rises steadily.

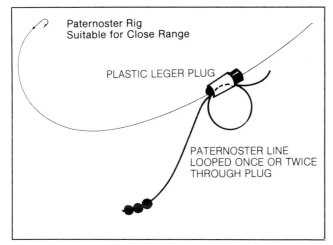

Paternoster Rig
Suitable for Close Range

PLASTIC LEGER PLUG

PATERNOSTER LINE
LOOPED ONCE OR TWICE
THROUGH PLUG

Fig 13

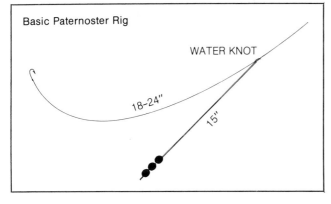

Basic Paternoster Rig

WATER KNOT

18–24"

15"

Fig 14

Ah, you say, but what about when a tench moves towards you, for it then gives no indication before it feels the lead? Well, that is another limitation of the method, though not as detrimental as it seems providing little lead is used. A similar take on a running rig almost certainly results in the lead being felt too, as I have explained, and in any case drop-back bites, which is what you get when a tench moves towards you and shifts the lead, usually result in a hooked fish.

But if the point still worries you neutral-buoyancy leger weights remedy the problem. You cannot buy them as far as I know, other than bubble floats, which work if you can find some, so you will need to make your own. The easiest way is to get hold of an old greenheart rod and cut sections from it in varying sizes from, say, one inch for close range, to three inches or more for longer casting. Greenheart usually sinks very slowly with no added ballast, and other hardwoods can be used, though differences in grain sometimes call for additional weight to get them just right. You can either drill a hole through the centre for the line, using plastic plugs or shot both sides to retain it, or glue in a wire loop or swivel. Another way is to partially hollow out the end of a balsa dowel then glue in an appropriate sized bomb. Varnishing will be necessary to seal the balsa.

Paternoster rigs are easily adapted to give long or short hook lengths, since the water-knot or plastic-plug junctions can be slid up and down the line – wetting the line first to avoid heat built-up by friction, which can break it. A variation I use is a long paternoster link of about 30 inches, with a very short hook link. A buoyant bait like crust is used, though other small baits such as maggot and caster can be made buoyant by sliding a small ball of poly-styrene (as used in packing) onto the hook shank, and lobs can be air-injected with a syringe. After casting, the tackle is tightened to the lead so the terminal rig lies in a straight line. The short hook link allows the bait to rise just above bottom, a presentation which tench like very much. The rig is particularly sensitive, the slightest touch being clearly registered on the indicator.

Long Range

Distance fishing is not one of my favourite ways of catching tench, but there is no denying its necessity on some waters. Those which are flogged every day, especially those containing a low stock

Len Head's indicators in use.

Excuse our backs – but one of the nice things about tench fishing is watching them swim free upon returning.

of specimens, are examples where long-range fishing might pay off, since the tench soon wise up and stay well out. Other waters may contain bottom features, weedbeds or food-holding areas far out.

Some tench fishers create a hotspot by continually fishing and baiting a distant area. If you put bait in a spot long enough some tench are going to be attracted to it, even if the swim has little else going for it. One or two good fish get caught, the word goes round, the next angler moves in and introduces more bait, then the next and so on till tench become conditioned to finding food there and a hotspot is created.

As a rule better and quicker success will be found by fishing a good bottom feature closer in, but hurling big leads towards the horizon has become something of a cult which many indulge in regardless of whether it is really necessary. I watched one angler casting a good ninety yards, nice accurate casting which placed his bait in a small tight patch. Trouble was, they were dropping into the water twenty yards from the opposite bank where he could have reached the same spot with an underarm swing!

I would say that anything over seventy or eighty yards is long range. Anglers talk glibly of catching tench at a hundred yards plus, but few really appreciate just how long a throw that is. Most who think they reach those targets would be lucky to make a measured seventy yards with bait. If you doubt that, get onto a field, measure out a hundred yards, then see how you get on.

However, providing an efficient casting style is used, the rod has sufficient power, the reel spool is filled to the lip, and a shock leader is used, tench a hundred yards away are catchable. A rod with fewer rod rings casts marginally further than one with a lot because of line friction through the rings. However, smooth retrieve with a fish on is spoiled by going to the extreme with too few, because the line, following sharp angles between the too widely spaced rings, gives a jerky recovery. I have found that six rings including the tip for a 12-foot rod gives the best of both worlds, the butt ring positioned about 30 inches above the reel seat.

Obviously one has to use a line diameter compatible with the size of fish expected and the existence of snags, but the lower the diameter the longer the cast. A shock leader must be used with low-diameter lines, long enough to allow at least half a dozen turns around the reel spool. I use a leader of 12 or 14lb BS and join it to the reel line with a Uni–knot. A Bimini hitch is the ultimate leader knot for strength, a devil to tie but worth it if you have the patience.

Stunted overhead thumps where the rod is held horizontal behind then brought over in a short arc can never achieve big

distances. If you lean well back with the rod extended behind you, you can accelerate it through a much wider arc and so build up more power. Accuracy is important. It is little use achieving a consistent eighty or a hundred yards but fanning the baited hook all over the place. It needs to drop into the same spot every time.

It is usually possible to sight along the direction of the cast and use an object on the far bank as a target. You can even place your own marker there, failing any other. Straight directional casting at a target is not difficult, but getting the same length of cast each time is, no matter how good you are. The remedy is to cast into the spot and then tie a marker such as a piece of white cotton onto the line at the reel. You then have only to ensure that the marker is in the same position to know that the bait is fishing in the right spot.

Putting your own marker in the swim is the surest way to accuracy – see Fig 15. I use a spare rod and after casting the marker into position I place the rod some distance along the bank with the tip submerged in order to lay the line as tightly as possible along the bottom and at a wide angle from the fishing position, so there is less chance of snagging it while fishing.

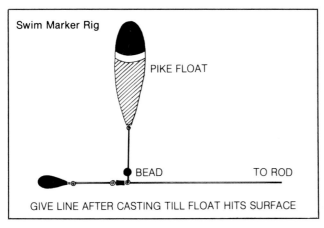

Fig 15

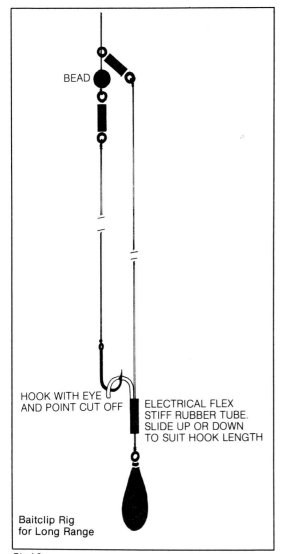

BEAD

HOOK WITH EYE
AND POINT CUT OFF

ELECTRICAL FLEX
STIFF RUBBER TUBE.
SLIDE UP OR DOWN
TO SUIT HOOK LENGTH

Baitclip Rig
for Long Range

Fig 16

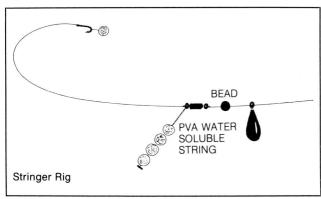

BEAD

PVA WATER
SOLUBLE
STRING

Stringer Rig

Fig 17

If you place the marker smack on the fishing spot you will snag it every time you cast, or a tench will do it for you. So position it a few yards further than you intend to fish then drop the baited hook that distance short. A problem with markers is that the necessary large float cuts down distance, at least on conventional gear. I have used shore fishing rods and 4oz leads when that was the only way.

End Rigs

The more bits and pieces there are on the terminal rig the more air resistance there is to defeat distance and accuracy, so keep end rigs simple. Big waters, long-range fishing, undertows and associated large bellies of line work against the efficiency of running-leger tackle unless a very big lead is used, so a paternoster may be considered better. However, powerful casting needs a slip-proof junction of the link to the main line, and I resort to a moulded metal ring, despite the extra knots. Casts are launched better by keeping the hook tail and link about the same length, though the hook tail can be an inch or two shorter to avoid tangles. A rig gleaned from shore fishing is a clip behind the lead to hold the bait in flight. Air resistance is minimised and the baited hook bumps free on impact with the water.

Do not fall into the long caster's mistake of perfecting distance and accuracy and then discovering that you are unable to get your groundbait out to the same spot. If you are using boilies, there should be no difficulty if you use a powerful catapult, resorting to a hunting-type sling-shot for real distance. Ideal-sized tench boilies are too small to fire great distances, whichever catapult you use, so it pays to increase the size a little. A 'stringer' rig as shown in Fig 17 is useful to get a group of baits lying around the hook bait, but they offer considerable air resistance in flight, cutting down the range.

Much the same comments apply to the 'Doppelganger', which inverts under slack line to deposit the bait directly below the spot where it lands – useful for particle baits such as maggots, casters, beans, hemp, etc.

The Baitsafe

Another gadget evolved from shore fishing was brought to my notice by John Holden. It is called the Baitsafe, a hollow, vaned, bomb-shaped capsule which houses the hook bait and several free samples, casts like a bullet, and opens by a release mechanism to release its contents upon impact with the water. Another big advantage is its tendency to aquaplane on retrieval up and over obstructions like gravel bars or weedbeds between angler and fishing spot. Casting weight can be varied between 2 and 7oz by adding or removing individual lead inserts which slot into the nose.

Early tests are impressive, the capsule flying far and accurately, though for extreme range a bomb still has the edge. However, where absolute range is not the prerequisite, I can foresee Baitsafes being used extensively in the near future for all sorts of species.

At ranges beyond about seventy or eighty yards I think you can forget cereal groundbaiting unless you can get afloat to take it out yourself. A specially modified remote-control boat incorporating a container and tipping mechanism would also do the business. A throwing-spoon will project balls of groundbait to about eighty yards, though practice is needed for accuracy. Some of the lads at Sywell used to be able to drop balls into lovely tight patches, but whenever I tried it more bait went either over me or into other people's swims than in my own.

Swimfeeder Fishing

Properly used, there is no doubt that feeders, popularised for tench fishing years back by Bob Church and his friends, are one of the deadliest of methods.

At one time feeders were notorious for bad flight in casting owing to crude design – they were just blunt plastic tubes, with or without end caps. Modern feeders are aerodynamic, and good casting models are made by Drennen, Thamesley, and Middy, among others. Some are dual-purpose, with removable end caps so that they can be used both open and block-end.

I keep lead loading to a minimum on feeders, using only enough to get the range. Strong undertows do mean more lead to prevent all being dragged along, though it is not at all unusual to get a take as the feeder is actually dragging. Loaded feeders can weigh anything up to 4oz or more, continual casting of which really punishes the line at a running leger stop so that you need to check it regularly. Running rigs are also prone to tangles.

Anyhow, the principles I have outlined on running legers and friction are equally applicable to feeders, so I prefer minimal lead and paternosters.

It may pay to dispense with lead altogether. Maggot-filled block-ends can be cast a surprising distance, and open-enders filled with cereal can be thrown a very long way indeed without lead. When the feeder empties there is hardly any resistance to a bite, and there are even occasions when taking off the lead means the difference between twitches and good runs.

Twitch bites are a problem where small baits, especially maggots, are used extensively in feeders, but some of the twitches come as the tench pushes the feeder about on the bottom. Tench soon get used to the idea that a splash on the surface signals the arrival of more food, and often they are onto it as soon as it hits bottom, bumping it about as they try to extract the contents. There have been occasions when tench have actually sucked out the contents of an open-ended feeder before it has even reached bottom. Then, tucking the hook bait inside the feeder succeeded in catching tench on the drop. You can time the descent of the feeder by letting it sink on a tight line – when it suddenly falls slack it has touched down. If it fails to fall slack when it should, strike!

When tench are homing in to a feeder quickly a short hook length often pays off – but not always, because cautious fish may drop the bait on feeling resistance. A longer tail is usually a better choice. A feeder dropping through the swim releases some of its contents on the way, creating a sprinkling of slowly sinking feed on top of it after it has settled. The bait on a long tail flutters down enticingly with it, giving a very natural presentation which often provokes a flying bite before you have had a chance to set the indicator.

My favourite rig is the 18-inch paternoster link and 15-inch hooklink. If you pull the tackle back a little after casting to straighten the rig, the hook bait is presented within inches of the feeder, yet there is plenty of resistance-free movement for the bite to develop.

Groundbait Cupping

At one time friends and I swung away from feeders in favour of cupping, and I cannot say we caught less tench by doing so. We designed various gadgets upon which a ball of stiff groundbait could be moulded without flying off the cast, and used the method just as we would feeders. The idea of cupping is that the groundbait quickly disperses to leave only the resistance of the gadget to a bite and in the retrieve – old-design feeders were awful things to wind in, kiting all over the place.

Making gadgets for cupping is obsolete with the recent introduction of the Thamesley Tackle 'Emmstat Crumb', a streamlined plastic cage-frame model with lead in the nose. It holds groundbait well providing the mix is stiff, and offers virtually no resistance on the retrieve. A limitation of our old prototype gadgets was that they would not take groundbait with maggot or caster in the mix because the ball broke up too easily, a shortcoming which does not apply to the Emmstat.

Casting accuracy is a point I seem to have emphasised a lot, but its importance is impossible to overemphasise and in feeder fishing can make all the difference between resounding success or total failure. I have explained that tench in many waters, particularly gravel pits, travel about in small groups. The object is to gather as

Casts fly further for long range by increasing the power with a lay-back casting style.

many of these groups into one spot as you can, and you cannot do that by spraying feederfuls of bait all over the place.

Markers to aim at help, and the longer the range the more vital they become. Long range when applied to feeder fishing is to me from fifty to seventy-five yards. It is possible to hurl a feeder further by resorting to really meaty tackle, but it takes all the fun out of it and in any case the method becomes increasingly inefficient the further you reach, until at extreme range it is no longer practical. I have yet to meet the angler who can place a feeder in the same spot every time, marker or not, at ranges beyond seventy yards.

At sensible range, powerful lay-back casting styles are not needed. An overhead cast can achieve the range and – more important – is more accurate. The best method is to hold the butt just above shoulder height with the rod horizontal behind you. Look at your marker whilst bringing the rod over your shoulder in an absolutely vertical (twelve o'clock) arc towards the target. The feeder will fly true towards the marker. Casting with the rod coming over at one or two o'clock invariably sends the tackle off course.

Specialised Tactics

Early-season tench and those in heavily populated waters rarely call for more advanced techniques than those so far covered. At other times the situation rapidly changes after the first couple of weeks; the bulging nets of naive fish become a rarity, and you find yourself having to work hard for every bite.

Anglers love to debate this dramatic change-round: 'they do not need our bait with the abundant natural food of mid-summer'; 'they are preoccupied on daphnia or bloodworms'; 'they turn predatory and feed on fry'. Rarely do you hear the view that it is due to the few weeks of intense angling pressure, during which most of the tench population has been either caught, lost, pricked or frightened and has simply become tackle-shy. Anglers tend to over-estimate wildly the tench population in a given lake. At times they see tench rolling all over, assume that there are loads more below, and refuse to accept that such large numbers could nearly all have been caught in those first couple of weeks.

In fact the trigger (whatever it is) that induces tench to roll can affect virtually the entire population of sizeable fish, and those seen rolling represent almost the entire stock. At other times you get a group of fish moving about the lake rolling as they go, and spectators again conclude that lots of tench must be responsible when in fact there are only a few.

So I believe that the cause of difficult fishing from early July is because the tench have become cagey. On more than one occasion I have fished later in the season at waters which had not so far been fished that year, finding tench every bit as co-operative as June fish on flogged waters, which tends to confirm my views.

Overcoming Tackle-shyness

I think the biggest single cause of tackle-shyness is the stiffness of the hook length, more specifically the few inches next to the hook. Heavy-wire hooks used with small or buoyant baits like flake are another cause. In both instances the bait does not behave in the same natural way as the groundbait upon which the tench has been feeding.

Picture a tench in the swim. It browses slowly about, raising small puffs of silt as it up-ends here and there to vacuum in, from about two inches away, a morsel of food. It tilts back to the horizontal, gills working faster as the food is taken back to the pharyngeal teeth, and, as it moves away the water displacement causes groundbait, maggots, bits of flake, boilies, or whatever to swirl about on the bottom.

The tench feeds on confidently, bubbling profusely and causing the angler on the bank to hover expectantly over the rod for the forthcoming bite. But his bait has already been rejected; the stiff nylon or heavy hook anchored the bait and prevented it from rising freely from the bottom as the tench tried to suck it in. Perhaps it did succeed in sucking it in but felt the line and spat it out again, probably causing a dip on the angler's float or a twitch on his indicator.

The chances are the last time the tench came across food that behaved that way it got caught, and it is not about to make the same mistake so easily. Scaling down the diameter of your hook-link line or using a finer-wire hook may do the trick. Better still, tie on a Dacron hook link. Dacron definitely gets more bites. It is thicker than monofil of the same strength but many times limper, so that movement of the hook bait is less restricted. I use spools of 3lb and 6lb BS which I dyed a muddy brown colour.

The wet strength of Dacron is considerably less than the stated BS. My 6lb line, for example, knotted and wet, breaks at 4½lb. It also has virtually no stretch so you

Pulling the line tight to the lead with a bolt rig before clipping into the rod clip.

need to compensate for that by using a reasonably elastic reel line to cushion the shock of striking.

Another dodge to fool tackle-shy tench is to scale right down to a fine hook link, but also incorporate a 6-inch length of pole elastic. The light hook link allows natural presentation but does not break during the fight because the elastic takes the strain. Playing tench on this rig feels most peculiar, with a sort of spongy yo-yo sensation as the tench bounces about on the elastic

Hair Rigs

Tench anglers should take their hats off to the thinking of carp men for the development of the hair rig, which is every bit as effective for tench as it is for carp. Kevin Maddocks and Lenny Middleton were the originators of the rig, perhaps the most brilliant legering innovation in recent years. The short length of very fine line allows near-perfect presentation of the bait, the fish takes confidently and the hook, which should be reasonably small and light, follows the bait into its mouth.

A follow-on from the original idea was to use very hard baits so that the carp passed them quickly back to the throat teeth for crushing – the hook thereby automatically following into the front of the mouth. In tench fishing with the hair rig hard baits work for the same reason, but bait consistency seems not quite so important and the rig works well with

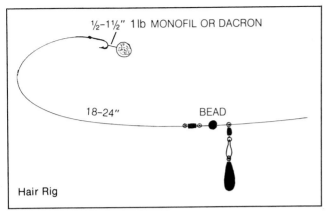

½–1½" 1 lb MONOFIL OR DACRON

18–24"　　　BEAD

Hair Rig

Fig 18

pastes and other soft baits. However, tench have a habit of rolling soft baits about in their mouths before taking them to the throat teeth so the hair should be kept short, about ¾ inch, to ensure that the hook is also in the mouth.

I find a standard length of 1 to 1¼ inches for harder baits to be right most of the time, but you may need to experiment on the day, or from water to water. If you hook a fish on the outside of the mouth the hair is too long, while a throat-hooked fish means it is too short. Remember that a really short hair defeats the object and if problems persist you may do better to alter the hook tail and/or lead link.

In due course tench become wary on any rig and may eject baits fished on the standard hair without taking in the hook. Try tying a shortish hair to the hook eye, or a slightly longer one to the line above it. Hook and bait then lie side by side so that in sucking in the bait the tench cannot help but suck in the hook too. A small light hook obviously increases the chances of this taking place, but in swims where you cannot risk small hooks a strip of polystyrene glued along the shank of a larger one gives it neutral buoyancy, helping to ensure it is easily vacuumed off the bottom along with the bait. With the correct

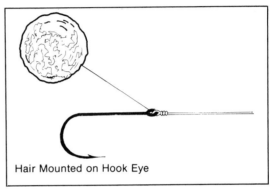

Hair Mounted on Hook Eye

Fig 19

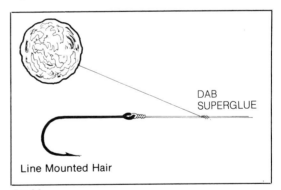

DAB
SUPERGLUE

Line Mounted Hair

Fig 20

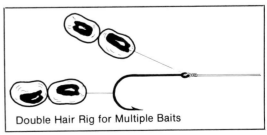

Double Hair Rig for Multiple Baits

Fig 21

ingredients a boilie can also be mixed to counterbalance the weight of the hook, so that together they just sink (see Chapter 16).

The tiny bites which occur on sweet-corn, maggots and other multiples in waters where they are extensively used can be transformed into good confident takes if the same baits are presented on a hair rig. Tench browsing on multiple baits are accustomed to sucking in several at one time if they happen to lie together on the bottom, and a good rig to imitate these free offerings is to use two hairs with one or two baits on each, one tied to the bend and the other to the eye of the hook or the line above it, where a dot of superglue will prevent it slipping.

Early publicity on hair rigs brought some concern that with the hook detached from the bait a lot of fish would be foul-hooked outside the mouth. In practice the fears have proved unfounded – at least where hairs of sensible length are used. I have caught hundreds of tench, many carp and other species too and can recall only three fish hooked outside the mouth, and odd fish are foul-hooked whatever rig you use. Should you encounter this problem with a hair tied to the hook bend, moving the hair to the eye or the adjacent line will remedy it, nearly all tench being hooked to one side of the bottom lip. What happens is that the tench sucks all in, feels the strangeness of the steel and attempts to blow the bait out. The hook, being heavier than the bait, hangs below it and catches the bottom lip as the tench tries to eject it.

A lightweight monkey climber made from one-inch diameter polyball and incorporating betalight.

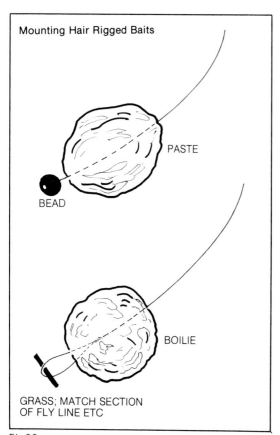

Mounting Hair Rigged Baits

PASTE

BEAD

BOILIE

GRASS; MATCH SECTION OF FLY LINE ETC

Fig 22

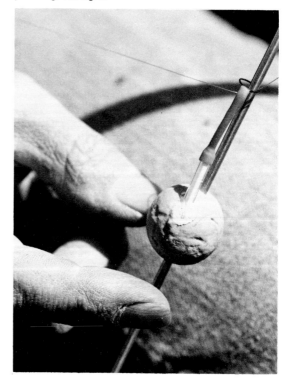

Bolt Rigs

It may seem an odd statement but I think that nowadays the hair rig is too well known. People are habitually using it regardless of the water, time of year, or how easy tench may be to catch on less sophisticated rigs. Most waters would benefit if the rig was saved as an ace to be resorted to only when fishing has become more difficult. Also, effective as it is, it still cannot totally imitate free offerings, and extensive use anywhere will ultimately lead to tench becoming wary, sucking in and blowing out even baits mounted on hairs.

The bolt rig was developed to counter this habit of sucking in and blowing out. Fig 23 shows a standard rig using a short hook link in conjunction with a large lead of from one to two ounces. The idea is that a fish picks up the bait, is pricked or feels resistance, and bolts, whereupon the hook

point finds a hold.

There are several ways to provide the resistance. One is to pull the line tight to the rod against the heavy lead and then clip it into a run clip attached to the rod. Another is to fix a backstop (a plastic leger plug) a short distance above the lead so that in taking a little line the fish hits the lead. The third method is to use a fixed, non-running lead. You are left in no doubt when a tench pricks itself on a bolt rig: the line simply hisses from the reel or, if you fish with the bale arm closed, the reel backwinds furiously. Drop-backs are common when using a fixed lead, while a back-stopped rig may result in a short pull-up followed by a drop-back. In both these cases a heavy indicator is needed to register the bite.

The size of the bait and hook combination is important since the success of the rig relies upon the hook point being in no way impeded. A larger hook than usual (or

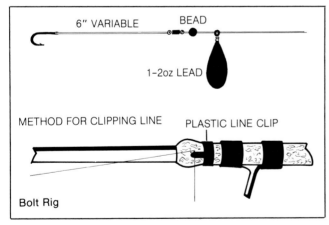

Bolt Rig

Fig 23

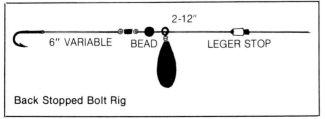

Back Stopped Bolt Rig

Fig 24

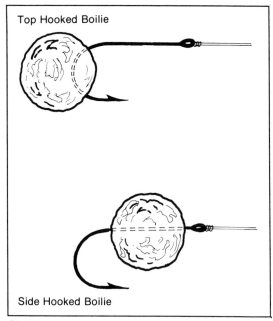

Top Hooked Boilie

Side Hooked Boilie

Fig 25

smaller bait), preferably with a wider gape, is used, and the bait is either nicked onto the bend (top-hooked) or slid up the shank against the eye (side-hooked). I usually side-hook, ensuring that there is a good gap between the edge of the bait and the hook point.

I must add that success with the basic bolt rig is nowhere so clear-cut with tench as it is with carp – for which it was devised – and sometimes a lot of juggling about is necessary before it works properly. The reason is that a tench takes a bait more gently than a carp, so there is less

of a jolt, and thus less tendency for it to be pricked and less likelihood of it bolting with the bait.

My early experiments with the rig illustrate the point. Using a six-inch hook link and line clip produced no takes, yet on winding in I found that the bait had been crushed. So I put on a backstop four inches above the lead and used a butt indicator without clipping up the line, which resulted in a four-inch pull. Obviously the tench had taken the free four inches, but too gently to prick itself as it came up against the lead. I moved the stop to two inches away, and got a two-inch lift, and when I moved it to one inch away – that's right – a one-inch pull! I began shortening the hook link, eventually resorting to a length of two inches with the backstop only two inches behind the lead, and began to get proper takes, the tench pricking themselves and bolting.

I have since found that the really short hook link with a side-hooked bait is, more often than not, the best method, but that the backstop may need adjustment between one and six inches, depending on the day and the water.

Bolt rigs are notoriously prone to tangling, the bait fouling the line behind the lead in flight. Doug Wood showed me an anti-tangle rig he used for carp when he wanted to allow a little free line before the carp felt the lead. With slight modifi-

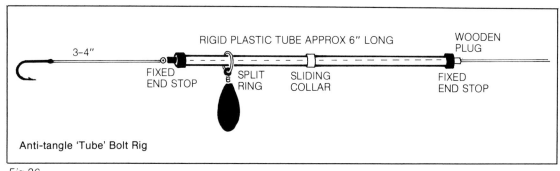

Anti-tangle 'Tube' Bolt Rig

3–4"   RIGID PLASTIC TUBE APPROX 6" LONG   WOODEN PLUG

FIXED END STOP   SPLIT RING   SLIDING COLLAR   FIXED END STOP

Fig 26

cations I have found it good for tench too. It incorporates a six to eight-inch length of stiff plastic tubing, with stops on both ends to retain a sliding lead which slides up and down the tube on a split ring. The tube is plugged tight to the line by a piece of match or cocktail stick pushed in one end, so that it slides freely through the split ring attached to the anchored lead when a fish takes.

I found that by adding an adjustable collar (a piece of aquarium air pipe) to the tube behind the lead I could easily alter the 'taking' length and thus cater for the whims of tench during a session. Providing the hook link is kept shorter than the length of the tube, tangles are virtually eliminated.

A very accurate if not powerful casting style, suitable for most feeder fishing.

Phil's Rig

I have always been unhappy using the large hook and small bait on bolt rigs, not because tench are scared of seeing the hook because they are not, but more because its heavy weight compared to the bait half anchors it so that it does not behave properly and might not be readily sucked in. Buoyant baits help of course, but my brother Phil came up with a neat idea which allows the use of a much smaller hook. His idea was to tie a short loop of shirring elastic to the shank. The bait is mounted as you would using a hair and the elastic pulls it tight to the hook shank. Phil 'grooves' a boilie bait so that the shank fits nicely in it with the hook projecting at right angles, leaving most of the bend and point clear with no chance of being impeded by the bait. I have found that pole elastic, being stretchier, is better than shirring, because it pulls the bait tighter to the hook shank.

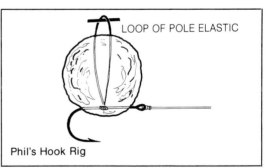

Fig 27

The Hair-bolt Rig

Perhaps the final resort is the hair-bolt rig, also devised for those times when fish have become wary of ordinary hairs. The bait is hair-mounted in the usual way but with a shorter hook link of about ten inches in combination with a run clip, backstop or fixed lead. It is a deadly combination for

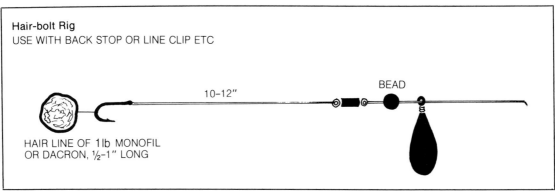

Fig 28

wary fish. I cannot help noticing, though, that like the standard hair rig many anglers are using the hair-bolt in a stereotyped fashion, as a first-choice method right from the off on all waters, in any conditions, quite regardless of whether the quarry have reached the wary stage or not.

If you cast out a boilie on a bolt or hair-bolt rig, clip the line up tight and turn the indicator volume to full blast, you are quite at liberty to have a kip until a tench comes along and hooks itself, roars off at 90 m.p.h. and wakens you so you can get up,

have a stretch, make a cup of tea, and then wind it in. It negates all that intense watching of the indicators, and the thrill of seeing one inch towards the butt ring as a tench takes. Why, you do not even have to go through the boring routine of striking!

And there is the rub, for most of the enjoyment of real tenching is totally lost. If numbers in the net are the only consideration then go ahead, but if, like me, you just like tench fishing, then save the self-hooking rigs for those days when they are the only option.

15 · Traditional Baits

An interesting point to emerge when browsing through annual lists of tench captures is that the majority are still taken on conventional baits. Perhaps that is not really so surprising; most tench are caught on traditional baits simply because most anglers still use them.

Broadly speaking, traditional baits lend themselves best to traditional methods – float fishing, weedbed swims, close-range work, etc. – while modern baits such as boilies slot perfectly into modern techniques using hair and bolt rigs, and at long range. That is obviously a simplification; there will be some overlapping. But you hardly ever see anyone bolt-rigging a freshwater mussel at eighty yards, or presenting a boilie on a lift rig.

I am often asked what is the best bait for tench, and I reply honestly that to the best of my knowledge there is no best bait. It is a mistake to consider baits in isolation anyway. It is not a matter of which *is* best, but which might work best on the day, the water, the swim, the mood of the tench, and the method you want to use.

When prospecting a new lake you may be told that it is a flake water, a worm water, or whatever, for tench in certain places do respond better to one bait than others. But while it is often wise to heed advice from regulars I know from experience that it pays to keep an open mind and to remain flexible in bait selection. If flake is the local bait but the water is not producing the quality of catches it seems capable of, then I would certainly choose

to try something different. Copying the methods of others who get unsatisfactory results means that your own results will probably be unsatisfactory too. Being different, not only with baits but in many other facets of tench fishing, is rarely unrewarding.

Flake

Flake is one of the big three tench baits,

Maggots; there is no finer bait to get tench rooting around in the swim.

along with worms and maggots. Between them, they account for more tench every year than all others put together. Not all small ones either – some very big fish come out to these three and one of my own best, a fish of 8lb 1oz, fell to flake. It is curious that flake is so good; after all, it is far from natural and without anglers tench are hardly likely ever to see any at all. I think it is the consistency of flake that makes it so good; its buoyancy disguises the weight of the hook so the bait behaves more naturally on the bottom. It is also highly visible and therefore more easily spotted by the short-sighted tench.

Flake is probably the most versatile of all baits. You can use large wodges on big hooks or small nips on little hooks; you can fish it hard on the bottom, as a slow sinker for midwater fish or to settle on top of silkweed, and also to flutter down to bubblers. I used to use the crumb from an uncut loaf but now favour a nip from a slice of medium-sliced loaf – the kind that looks (and tastes) like damp blotting paper.

Some people mould flake onto the hook so that it thuds to the bottom, where it sits like an uninviting chunk of stodge. Even if it is taken the point of the hook is masked and fails to go home. Much better to tear off a slice, double it, squeeze it in the middle, then push the hook point through the 'squeeze'. My brother Ted used to conceal the whole hook without masking the point by doubling a piece over it and then nipping it round the edges. He called it an apple turnover.

While flake can be good anywhere, it seems particularly reliable on some clear-water lakes, for reasons which are unclear, unless it is that its natural presentation allays the extra caution of tench living in these crystal-clear waters. It is also good when fishing holes and clearings in weed-beds, and invaluable when you need to offer a bait on top of bottom weed. In one swim I recall a dense forest of Canadian pondweed grew in seven feet of water but stopped 18 inches below the surface, forming a sort of weed plateau over which tench had the habit of emerging at intervals from a hole on one side, crossing over the plateau, then disappearing through a gap opposite. A big wodge of fluffy flake settled on top of the forest and was taken by the first fish to cross, followed by several more – an instance when flake proved indispensable.

Perhaps the one failing of flake is its (to us) lack of smell. But flavouring it gives the best of both worlds, providing a visible bait that is buoyant and smelly too. I went through a spell when I did well after smearing my flake bait with curry paste, and other flavours have increased its effectiveness. I add flavour by diluting 1,000-to-1 strength carp flavourings with 50 per cent water and spraying a squirt from an atomiser. A home-baked loaf could incorporate any flavour in the mix.

Another dodge which works is to spray on a tiny squirt of undiluted concentrated sweetener. This has given a new lease of life to flake on hard-fished waters, but a temporary one, because tench appear to get wise to very sweet flake quickly. A change to another additive usually gets things moving again. There have been plenty of tench caught on flake flavoured with maple, almond, butterscotch, vanilla, and green zing, though others would probably prove equally good.

Crust

There are days in tench fishing, those dog days when nothing seems to work, when crust catches after all else has failed. Like flake, perhaps its natural buoyancy does the trick. But the reason is not so important; it is enough to know that there are times when it works and when those times are.

Crust has scored when tench have been preoccupied on some natural food item, bubbling away but ignoring all hook baits until a tiny fragment of crust on a small hook was presented two inches off bottom on an overdepth float leger rig, with the tackle tightened till a mere suggestion of tip showed. A zone of preoccupation is a hive of activity when several tench are at it. Puffs of silt, debris and food are swirled into suspension. Sometimes tench probe deep into the silt ignoring anything on top, yet pausing now and then to pick off any

The lips of tench are semi-protusible, the better to suck in food items while inches away.

food items floating in suspension. Those are the times when the crust fragment, anchored to float off bottom, can be the answer.

Crust also perfectly complements the lift rig. Fred J. Taylor's recommendation of its use years ago is as valid today as it was then.

The natural buoyancy of the bait can be used to complement any other method where you want an off-the-bottom presentation or feel that the weight of the hook is putting tench off. Maggots, worms, etc., can all be offered at any depth off the bottom or made to sink as slowly as you choose. Cocktails often work even when to us they could hardly appear more unnatural, for example a crust-lobworm combination 18 inches off the bottom which accounted for a near six-pounder

fifteen years ago – at the time a monster and my personal best.

Tench patrolling along a regular beat can swim straight past a hook bait lying in a groundbaited patch, yet accept 'on the run' a lone large bait such as crust hovering in its path just above the bottom.

Compressed flavoured crust has proved to be really good. Cut the crust from the sides of a sandwich loaf, then soak two cloths in a solution of diluted flavouring. Ring out the surplus, place the cloth on a flat surface with the crust arranged on top, cover with the second cloth and on top of that place a weighty flat board. Twenty-four hours later you have a superb semi-buoyant tench bait.

One night vigorous slurping in a reeded margin prompted me to investigate with a torch. Before the beam put them down, the torch picked out several tench which had been sucking at slices of bread thrown in by the day anglers, confirming what I already knew, that in many waters, carp waters especially, tench will feed and are catchable on top – especially close in, after dark, on the bank into which the wind was or is blowing. Tench similarly feed on other carp fishers' leftovers, such as floating cat and dog foods.

Paste

Bread paste is nowadays a neglected bait, yet it can be a superb and versatile one. One good angler I know, Arthur Russell, rarely uses much else, and his results are proof enough that its non-use elsewhere is unjustified. I need not describe how to make it other than to remind you that stale bread makes the best paste, and, despite lots of tench coming out on other hard baits, that it needs to be soft.

Plain paste is good, but you can also flavour it and otherwise use it as a base for other additives and ingredients. You can sweeten it by adding caster sugar or liquid concentrate sweetener, and you can use it as a cocktail with maggot, caster, or whatever. I recall another phase when casters pushed into a hook bait of soft paste produced more takes than anything. Bangers and mash, we called it. Rolling a paste ball in hemp produced an excellent alternative.

The first tench I ever caught took paste into which I had kneaded custard powder to produce a yellow bait. The excellence of yellow baits was known by my grandfather and his before him, for custard powder is an ancient additive for tench baits. Perhaps, though, they did not realise that the vanilla flavour in custard played its part.

Smell, taste, colour and consistency in a bait are important in that order. Paste lends itself perfectly to experiment, the search for that ideal blend – perhaps an orange or yellow sweetened soft paste, lightly flavoured with a water soluble additive like butterscotch, maple, or caramel. There is nothing new in these ideas. Read this from the Revd Daniels's *Rural Sports*, written in 1801.

Red paste may be made with a large spoon of wheat flour moistened with white of egg, worked until tough, add small quantity of honey or loaf sugar finely powdered, together with cotton wool, colour with a little vermilion, fresh butter added prevents it becoming hard. Make yellow by mixing Turmeric.

Worms

If I could use only one bait, worms would

be my choice without hesitation. They are the universal tench bait and I have never, ever, fished a water where tench cannot be caught on them. Odd waters have needed a little more time, but always the fish respond in the end. I will go further and state that if you take a thousand worms, three sessions, and a good angler, tench can be caught from any water, anywhere.

I do not claim that they are always the best bait, but I do claim that the most difficult water can be cracked, given time, with good lively worms for hook bait and – most important of all – lots more to chop up and mix with cereal to prebait a swim.

Worms are almost as versatile as paste. A big one makes a good mouthful so you can fish without being continually pestered by small fry. And a good lobworm is weighty enough for accurate freeline casting to bubblers, yet in the water sinks slowly enough to be very attractive as it drifts down before the tench's nose. An air-injected worm presented from two inches to a foot or more above bottom is deadly, particularly when it is given periodic tweaks through the swim.

Anglers argue about whether a tench takes a worm head or tail first, and therefore where to insert the hook to avoid missed bites. Having watched plenty of tench take them I can tell you that they are indiscriminate about unhooked offerings – they take whichever end of a big worm they bump into first. A small worm, sometimes even a lob, disappears in one gulp, but large ones are usually sucked an inch or two in and chewed before the rest follows in one or two more gulps. Whatever the size of the worm, it may be sucked in and blown out several times before it is swallowed. However, tench do differentiate between the free end and that with the hook in it.

It is common, after missing a bite, to find the tail end of a head-hooked worm chewed. Changing the hookhold to the tail end often results in chewed head ends. I do not like tandem-hook rigs; in any case they have never cured the problem. Lob tails will probably do the trick.

BLUEHEADS

Only a few of the large variety of breeds of worm are of real interest to tench fishers. Most anglers rate lobworms the best, but blueheads – a tougher, rounder variety growing to about six inches with, as its name implies, a blue-black head – are superior. Given that the hook bait is lively (an important business with any worm), blueheads have always outfished lobs. Perhaps they taste better – something I have never found out for myself.

Blueheads are more difficult to find than lobs. They rarely come to the surface after dark, so you need to dig them up from soil with a fairly high clay content. Potato patches are good, even without clay.

MARSH WORMS

Marsh worms are almost as good as blueheads, if not equally good, but they are even more difficult to find. They resemble big redworms, growing to about four or five inches, with a fatter body and a purplish iridescent sheen. The liveliness is part of their attraction; you can fish for several hours and still wind one in wriggling. Digging in marshy fields or banksides, under fallen branches and other damp areas usually unearths enough for hookbait, though you would be fortunate to find enough for groundbait too.

LOBWORMS

And that's where lobworms come in, because the ease of gathering large

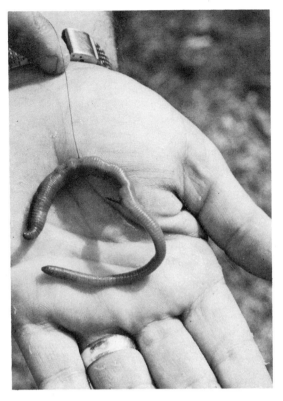

Lobworms need hooking just once; place the hook a third of the way down from the head.

numbers from the lawn after dark on mild damp nights makes them ideal for groundbait – you certainly need plenty. Chopping worms for groundbait is a tedious and messy game, made easier if you drop them onto the top of the crumb and use a large pair of scissors.

Enough tench are caught on lobs to prove that they are a good hookbait too, provided they are lively. A limp, bedraggled half-dead lob looks about as unappetising to a tench as it does to us. Most of the year I keep a good supply of lobs by storing them in an old-fashioned tin bath filled with a mixture of soil, leafmould, and damp newspaper.

Most anglers know well enough that lively worms are better than dead ones, but

I wonder how many realise that at a certain stage of decomposition dead lobs can outfish live ones. I first discovered this years ago during an eel-fishing session, when I had neglected to keep my worm box out of the sun and they all over-heated and died.

Those dead worms took eels one after another while all around the lively baits of others remained untouched. In due course one of them baited up from my box, and he too was quickly into an eel. Subsequent experiences with tench as well as eels have reinforced my original findings, and I can only assume that, at this critical stage, the dead worms exude a particularly attractive scent or blend of amino-acids. That critical stage is hard to obtain by design; I have tried and failed most times. Worms in the right condition do not yet smell, are firm and dry, and have become bloated at the head end. A steady build up of heat in an airtight box is the nearest I can get to the magic treatment. If you discover a better way I do hope you will let me know.

REDWORMS AND BRANDLINGS

True redworms are superb. They work particularly well in winter because, however cold the water, they remain lively on the hook. Redworms are often confused with brandlings, those similar-sized worms with yellow bands and pungent scent, which are nowhere near as good as true reds and are greatly overrated for tench – and other species, too, in my experience.

Both types are found in well rotted manure and compost heaps, with brandlings far more prolific than reds. Really old horse manure heaps are worth poking about in for reds. Chicken manure is also good.

Maggots

Analysis of catch reports in and out of the press shows that maggots catch more tench than any other bait. Their easy availability, lack of preparation, and ease of feeding the swim make them the most widely used bait of all, and one would expect the bait which is used most to catch most tench – taken nation-wide. So the results are biased, and it is tempting to conclude that lots of tench are caught in spite of, rather than because of, maggots.

I too have caught many tench on them and cannot dismiss them easily. There is no other bait more guaranteed to get tench rooting about in a swim than a carpet of maggots, and, while they will accept a bunch on a decent-sized hook, few better hook baits either. But anyone who regularly fishes maggots soon finds that bunches no longer produce, and has to scale down to singles or doubles on small hooks. Bites deteriorate from runs to short pulls, and eventually to almost indiscernible twitches.

There are ways to turn twitches into hittable bites as explained elsewhere. But you limit your options, swim choice is in danger of centring on where you can play a strong fish on light tackle without losing it, rather than where you would expect most tench to feed.

I may seem to be suggesting that maggots are an excellent bait while advocating that you should not use them. That is not so. There are waters which respond particularly well to their use – open, fairly weed-free pits and lakes where maggots on the hook in conjunction with swimfeeders are deadly. What I am advocating is that tench anglers should not persist in using maggots once bites have turned to tweaks, unless of course you

enjoy what we used to call the 'tench fisher's twitch' – an affliction whereby the unfortunate angler turns progressively into a neurotic, jabbering simpleton, with eyes like chapel hat pegs from staring for, swatting at, and continually missing tiny movements on the indicator.

Down below, tench are moving just inches to pick up each free maggot, and if one takes those containing the hook the bite registration will be tiny unless the tench moves off. And wary fish reject the hook bait because it does not behave the same as all the free maggots. Even if it is taken it is likely to be rejected immediately. A tench blows out a suspicious bait with considerable force, and often the twitch you see on the indicator is the result of the bait being blown out, not being sucked in. The strike misses because the hook is not even in the tench's mouth.

It is much better to change baits when fishing becomes so difficult. When given that advice, anglers in danger of developing tench fisher's twitch look aghast and reply that it is impossible to get bites on other baits – their tench have become totally preoccupied with maggots. That is nonsense. Anyone with the problem should try a few sessions prebaiting with lots of chopped worms, and would then find the tench much less preoccupied.

Clean, soft maggots outfish stale smelly ones every time. Judging by the quality of bait I see used, few tench anglers seem to attach much importance to this point. Shop-bought maggots need cleaning by riddling two or three times through bran moistened with a little milk, and it is well worth the effort to breed large softer specials like gozzers for hook bait yourself. White maggots are as good as any colour, though I recall a period on Beeston Lake in Norfolk when Phil did well on red ones, perhaps imitating the profusion of blood-worm in the Beeston silt.

Flavoured maggots are all the rage. They certainly work and can give a new lease of life when tench have reached the twitchy stage on ordinary maggots. You can add the flavour to the bran whilst riddling, or smear some around the bait box with a piece of cotton wool. I just open the box, give them a couple of squirts with an atomising spray, give the box a good shake, and let them get on with it. It seems as good a way as any because in a while all the inhabitants are equally smelly. Pineapple, vanilla, strawberry, butterscotch and maple have all worked, as would other flavours.

Casters

Casters are one of the very best tench baits but are still underrated. In the seventies Bures Lake contained some very large tench which were extremely hard to catch. The lake pulsed with life of all the kinds tench like to eat, and many were the baits I failed to catch those tench on. Odd fish fell to bread, corn and maggot. Even prolonged baiting with worms failed to produce satisfactory results.

But one day I had thrown some old floating casters into the water, and as they drifted out on the ripple I saw tench sipping them in – just like trout. At last I had found, albeit accidentally, a bait that tench would accept, so I started baiting a swim and began catching tench, including the big ones, regularly. Tench in other waters since have shown a definite liking for casters – sometimes, as at Bures, when all else has failed.

Despite their success I do not recommend casters as a first-choice bait, but one to hold in reserve should fishing become difficult. There are two reasons: first, good fresh casters are not easily available and are costly in the quantities needed. Never bait a swim with casters which have gone off, or you will ruin the swim for some days. Second, fishing casters effectively demands the use of fine tackle, and most swims prohibit that because of weed growth.

You may get tench going on casters at the first baiting, but sometimes they will not respond until you have put bait in for a couple of days. I loose feed about two pints for the first session, reducing to a pint per session once tench are on them. Once tench are feeding confidently casters remain productive for a long time, much longer than maggots. Bites are usually bolder too. I think that tench like them so much that greed takes over and they feed more vigorously, giving better takes.

Although I did catch some large tench on casters after failing on other baits, they are not selective for big fish. All sizes of tench like them. However, catching big tench is about fishing the right water and then mostly about numbers. You find a method and bait which produce lots of tench, and sooner or later a big one will be among them.

Sweetcorn

It is curious that while corn works from the word go on some waters there are others where it will not work unless lengthy prebaiting is carried out, and some where it will not work at all. Where it does work it can be deadly, though its effectiveness is often short-lived, depending on the numbers of tench and how much corn is used.

Opposite   *The scales say it all – 6lb 2oz.*

With heavy use its effectiveness may last only a couple of weeks or less. When bites dry up it is not because tench have stopped eating corn but because of the old problem of the bait with a hook in it being heavier and not behaving like all the free offerings. Persistence in the use of corn usually brings short, rapid pulls when a tench bolts at its own bravado after sucking in what it knows it should not touch. You may hit one in three if your reflexes are sharp enough, but such bites are rarely frequent, generally catching you off guard so that you strike thin air.

In clear water swims you can put in a can of corn, finish the session with no bites, then discover that every grain has gone save the bit with your hook in it. Hair and bolt rigs go part way to solving the problem, as will a small ball of polystyrene slid onto the hook shank with the bait, which counters the weight of the hook. Flavouring and dying the bait a different colour, such as orange or red, also prolongs its effective life.

A dodge which I use in heavily corn-fished waters is to forget about putting in any loose feed at all. Pick a swim frequently fished but where tench have had time to clear up the previous angler's feed. Then cast out the hook bait only. This usually results in a confident take, from which I conclude that the very sight of a carpet of corn sets the alarm bells ringing, whilst a single grain in isolation poses no threat and is taken. The same objective is achieved by baiting a swim the day before fishing, but introducing no feed on the following day when you fish.

When prebaiting over a period before fishing, liberal baiting pays. However, it is a mistake to overfeed during the session whether tench have become wary of corn or not. One can is ample for a full morning.

Try a couple of catapult pouchfuls to start with, followed by half a dozen grains now and then, depending upon the amount of activity in the swim.

Friends report good results by using liquidised corn bound with a little crumb to form a sloppy groundbait as feed, with a whole kernel on the hook. The slop produces a milky, smelly cloud without overfeeding the fish. You can liquidise your own, but the cans of corn purée available from shops are as good and more convenient.

Freshwater Mussel

At one time I believed mussels to be the only bait that would select bigger tench, since on the first two waters I tried them they certainly took better than average fish and few small ones. I have since changed my mind, or at least I have concluded that it does not always apply, since I have taken lots of smaller tench on them from other waters.

Even so, I rate mussels highly for tempting big, wary tench, and they almost always produce nice confident bites. They are, after all, a totally natural bait. Strangely, it is not essential for the water to contain mussels for them to work, neither is it always necessary to prebait on such waters with free samples. However, best results do come if chopped up pieces are introduced before fishing. I throw in the empty shells as well, believing that things then appear more natural to the tench.

I would expect to use about a dozen mussels for one session, including hook bait. Swan mussels are usually plentiful in alkaline waters, as are duck mussels, which are equally suitable but more localised in distribution. Open them by inserting a

Insert a knife blade at the back of the shell, cut the hinges, and the fresh-water mussel will open.

knife blade and cutting the hinges at the back of the shell. I have caught plenty of tench on whole mussel, but I usually use a piece of the firmer yellow 'foot' for the hook bait.

The best spots to find them are in silty rush-lined margins, though they are also found in open water with a soft bottom. I have a specially made mussel harvester for the job which needs only a couple of pulls through to obtain plenty. I have seen mussels harvested to near-extinction when they were the going bait, so please do not denude your water. Mussels are slow-growing creatures and can take a long time to recolonise if they are thinned too severely.

Other Baits

Stewed wheat is a good but little-used bait. At one time popular, it has now fallen out of favour. Stewed wheat is exactly that – wheat stewed until it is soft. You do not need much because it swells enormously, and it is very easy to overfeed if you put too much in. Wheat is not unlike corn in that it may have a short life. However, while corn can be an instant bait wheat invariably requires prebaiting before it is freely accepted. Wheat lends itself perfectly to experiment by flavouring and dying – something I regret I have never got round to.

Freshwater snails ought to be deadly; tench certainly eat plenty where they are abundant. But my own attempts to catch tench with them have failed dismally and I

am forced to conclude they are of negligible value as a bait.

Similar comments apply to other natural
water creatures such as caddis grubs,
shrimps, damsel and dragonfly larvae and
fish baits. All have caught tench on odd
occasions but I cannot take them seriously
and regard their use as a bit like fly fishing
for tench – all right for the occasional light
flirtation but not to be expected to produce consistent results.

What else? Cheese can be excellent. So
can sugar puffs, cornflakes, berries, maca-
roni, noodles and most things edible, for
tench are catholic in taste. Little green
caterpillars shaken off hedgerows have
been known to be good, and any other land
creature that creeps or crawls is worth a
try when the going gets tough, but all are
relatively unimportant compared with the
main baits discussed.

16 · Modern Baits
Tench Baits for the Eighties

ROD HUTCHINSON

When discussing baits for tench the first thing that springs to mind is: What don't they take? Probably every variety of seed or flavoured paste or boilie intended for carp has at some time put old *tinca* on the bank.

I was discussing the subject with my fishing mate Brian Hankins, who has a lot of big tench to his credit. I offered the opinion that tiger nuts were about the only bait not to produce tench, only to be informed that tench had been taken on them at Savay Lake. 'But', added Brian, 'they certainly do not like peanuts much' – to which I replied that I had taken several one evening from our local lake on maple-soaked peanuts. It is obvious that from time to time tench will eat practically anything.

Brilliant tench baits can be made using modern flavours and ingredients.

Indeed, it is not uncommon during the opening months of the season to land tench which have numbers of fry in their throats. I well remember one balmy June evening when I took several tench in succession with lip-hooked minnows intended for some big perch in a local gravel pit, so even live and deadbaits cannot be discounted. And, although tench are rightly considered as primarily a bottom-feeding species, I have lost count of the numbers I have had over the years on floating crusts intended for carp. For many years the largest tench I had caught fell to a single floating caster fished on very fine tackle with a matchstick for a float. On that occasion the intended quarry had been large roach. Curiously, although I have spent several years fishing specifically for tench, all my best specimens have come while I was pursuing other species.

It is obvious from the vast range of baits that have put tench on the bank that the fish is very adaptable and will turn any abundance of food of whatever variety to its advantage. When carp anglers hammered in their particle baits in the mid-seventies it did not take long for tench to recognise this new bonanza of food. And when the fashion changed at the end of the decade to small boiled paste baits (boilies), the tench were as grateful as ever, so much so that scaled-down carp tactics – mass baiting and the use of bolt rigs – are now the accepted method for tench fishing on many waters.

The question is not which baits tench will eat, but which they would prefer. Correspondence I have been involved in suggests that in the majority of lakes flavours based on maple and vanilla are the best tench catchers, with straight maple extract and Maplecreme among the most popular, while blends with cream, butter-scotch, caramel, vanilla and barley sugar have all produced outstanding catches.

One interesting point is that most anglers find that flavours work better with tench used at higher levels than the average carp angler would use. I believe this is because of the poor eyesight of tench compared with carp. Tench grub for their food, and, even in rich gravel pits where their diet ranges from bloodworms to crustacea and molluscs, the items they feed on are generally static, and are found very much by feel and smell. For this reason a very powerful-smelling boilie will be detected much more quickly than one with little smell. Certainly it appears that flavour dosages of about 15 ml to a pound of base mix are most likely to score.

I have also found the past couple of seasons that a 'pop-up' boilie – one baked after boiling so that it floats – will be picked up much quicker than one fished on the bottom. On my local lake I can virtually guarantee a take from a tench within five minutes of casting out during the summer, providing the buoyant bait is anchored two inches off the bottom with a swan shot. I believe the tench move into the swim on hearing (or feeling the vibrations of) free baits entering the water. They know that food is in the area and because of their limited eyesight the bait rising off the bottom is the first one they find.

Others may disagree, but I find tench probably the least shy of all species. Indeed, they are probably the first to investigate water disturbance – be it dragging a swim or pelting it with groundbait or free offerings of boilies or particles. You can be pretty sure tench will soon be in there on the lookout for food. Capitalise on this with a strong-flavoured food supply and you are onto a winner. This gives the fish an additional target to home in on, counteracting their poor eyesight.

With these points still in mind, I am a firm believer in the use of groundbait (as distinct from free baits) for tench. A carpet of fine particles of food in an area is something a tench can hardly miss when it goes down to feed, despite the lack of visual appeal. Although it might appear contradictory considering that in the majority of waters sweet and creamy baits are favourites, in the experience of myself and friends fish-meal carpets cannot be bettered for drawing in and keeping fish in the swim. White fish-meal, sardine meal, and Codlivine (a vitamin supplement derived from fish offal) are all excellent additives used in conjunction with cereal or breadcrumb. One acquaintance swears by the following formula: one part white fish and one part Catchum Seafood Blend mixed with half a pint of water and two tablespoons of pilchard oil. The resulting groundbait is very sticky and smells to high heaven, yet his results certainly demonstrate the mixture does the trick.

This liking for fish-meal bases seems more pronounced in waters of high pH values. This type of water is usually identified by crystal-clear water and lush weed growth. In the vast majority of cases the lakes in question are relatively new (under twenty years) gravel workings. It has often been the case in this type of water that fishy-flavoured hook baits outscore the sweeter variety. Crayfish, salmon, lobster and prawn are the most popular flavours. It is by no means certain, but very probable, that this is due to the natural diet of tench in such an environment, which will be mainly crustacea and molluscs. These creatures contain organic acids which are used in the making of the flavours named.

Flavours apart, when tench are the quarry I am a firm believer in quality base mixes. In the type of water just mentioned, where the tench grow large, their natural diet is very high indeed in protein. Big fish need good food to sustain their weight and for this reason I would go for high nutritional bases every time. I think it is debatable whether or not this can be achieved best by the use of milk and soya proteins, or by the use of fish-meals, as some waters seem to respond to one better than another. Whichever is chosen, I feel, will be better than the carbohydrate 'carrier' type bases used on many carp waters.

Yet, however much we theorise about bait, there is always the fact that, natural

Rod Hutchinson is a legend within carp fishing, but no slouch with other species as this near 6lb tench reveals.

food apart, when it comes to hook baits fish can only eat what they are given. Even a relatively poor nutritional food source is going to be eaten if it is present in abundance. It is simply an easy larder. This gives rise to the great success one can have with tench when using particle baits.

Just as baits fished off the bottom work quickest because of their visibility, so it is with particles. Apart from two exceptions which I will deal with later, the more visible a particle is the better. Yellow and orange are without doubt the most instant of colours. Sweetcorn, yellow peas and lupin seeds (which are like giant yellow smarties) are all brilliant baits. The latter two work best when they have been soaked in a solution of one of the creamy flavours – butter, cream, Scopex, butterscotch or Maltrex – for twenty-four hours. Ideally, cover one pound of the seeds with three inches of water to which you have added 10 ml of the flavouring. After twenty-four hours, during which time most of the water will have been soaked up, put them in a pan, cover them with one inch of water and add another 5 ml of the flavouring. In the case of lupin seeds, which have a very bitter taste, add 5 ml of sweetener as well. After bringing them to the boil, turn down the heat and simmer for twenty minutes. They are then ready to use, or you can freeze them for another time.

One of my favourite tench baits is black-eyed beans. These are soaked and cooked in a similar manner, but instead of adding liquid flavouring just add one packet of Knorr tomato soup to the water before boiling. The resulting beans, besides having a rich tomato flavour, also end up a highly visible orange colour.

An exception to this visibility rule is maple peas, with which I have had exceptional tench action at that 'private water near Sevenoaks' which has been so prolific since the mid-seventies. I tend to fish maples differently from visible particles, by baiting on the little-and-often principle rather than expecting the fish to see a visible carpet. I am certain in my own mind success is due to the disturbance of baiting, because maple peas, being much denser than most particles, make quite a noise on hitting the water, which draws the fish in.

As a point of interest maples are the only particle on which I have caught carp, tench, roach and rudd on the drop. I think this bears out my belief that fish come to the sound of the bait hitting the water. Incidentally, I find that maples work best when no flavour at all is added. Simply soak, boil, and simmer for twenty minutes, and do not be afraid if they go off a bit and start emitting a milky fluid. In my experience this is when they are at their best for both tench and carp.

I hope that these notes will be of use to all anglers with tench in mind, but I should point out that there are no hard-and-fast rules. There is no way of telling if a water responds to sweet or fishy type baits without wetting a line. In the end, it is down to the individual angler, but I hope these few pages will provide food for thought, and maybe one or two of you will think, 'I will have to try that next year.'

*   *   *

As always when Rod Hutchinson talks about baits, he does indeed give food for thought, and he has one or two ideas which I may well try myself next year.

Rod notes that tench are quick to capitalise on any food source if it is abundant, and I agree that if enough is put in over a period tench will respond. Rod's minnow-caught

Ingredients need accurate and consistent weighing for each bait batch.

tench and my own experiences with tench regurgitating perch fry are examples of an abundant food supply being exploited even though it appears contrary to the usual dietary preference of tench.

Flavours

Providing it is present in sufficient quantity, almost anything edible will be exploited. However, I again agree that it is not so much a matter of what they will accept but of what they would prefer, and there is little doubt that some flavours work better than others. I also think that we ought to consider not only the flavour itself but which solvent has been used in its manufacture, whether alcohol or glycerol

types. Alcohol flavours are more volatile and leach more rapidly into the water, and with some you can find that after about thirty minutes' submersion no trace of the flavour remains. Those with a glycerol base hold the flavour longer; it diffuses slowly, and a bait can still smell strongly after even twenty-four hours or more in the water.

Knowing this can help baiting strategy. For instance, if a long prebait is under way you need to be sure that the baits will still smell attractive should they remain uneaten for a few days, which may happen in adverse feeding conditions. It would help if the flavour diffuses slowly, allowing the scent to linger a long time, so that tench get conditioned to the smell. In these cases slow-dissolving glycerol flavours make sense. However, should you be out for a short session on a water where tench are already accustomed to finding little round balls of various flavours, a fast dissolver would score better, making alcohol the better vehicle, and regular renewal of the hook bait would be sensible.

Many anglers fail to consider the taste of the flavouring as well as the smell. I have said that the receptors of tench probably 'taste a smell'. That being so, we should develop the habit of the finger test before choosing new flavouring. Dab a spot on your finger and taste it first; you may find that it smells good but tastes horrible. Also some flavours mixed with the same solvent may smell different but all taste the same – reason enough for tasting as well as sniffing. Alcohol flavouring usually has a bitter taste, which needs the addition of a sweetener, while glycerol types taste milder.

Bait dealers do not generally specify which solvent is used in the flavouring they sell. Many are tried and proven anyway, for example those mentioned by Rod, and you will get good results without knowing the solvent. But I would always ask before trying any new flavour.

Rod comments on the likelihood of fishy flavours working best on waters where tench feed predominantly on crustaceans. If that is so, I would expect natural flavours such as fish and shrimp meals and fish oils, both in groundbait and hook bait, to outscore synthetic ones. Synthetic flavours are, obviously, artificial – they are not the real thing. Therefore a smell which seems fishy to our nose only seems so, and to a tench is probably anything but (even though it may still attract them). In other words, if you use a flavour labelled 'Great Pond Snail' or whatever, you would be wrong to assume that it smells like snail to a tench.

Synthetic or not, there is no denying the effectiveness of many different flavourings. Those Rod mentions have proven track records and can be vouched for by successful tench anglers everywhere. Some, like butterscotch, nectar, seafood, maple and salmon, I too have been successful with; butterscotch was probably the best, especially when blended with another creamy flavour. Others I or my friends have used are honeycomb, strawberry, almond, bun spice, lemon and honey, and green zing, the last a close second to butterscotch blends.

The next step along from synthetics is more experimentation with other natural flavours such as essential oils. I have used a few with encouraging results. And there are notable instances where their use has been deadly on waters bombarded for a long time with synthetic flavours.

Essential oils are extremely concentrated and you need very little in a bait. The first time I tried geranium oil I used 10ml in a pound mix, and my mates could

smell it 150 yards along the bank. I blanked! About 2ml to a pound is ample, and even then may be too much if the oil is particularly strong.

Oils are insoluble in water and cannot freely leach from the bait, defeating the whole object of an attractant. Emulsifying additives are available from some bait suppliers and help to render the oils soluble, but they are only partially effective. The flavour manufacturers Dubuis & Rowsell Ltd, Duroma Works, Elmwood Road, Croydon, Surrey, do supply a solvent for their own range of oils which renders them completely miscible in water.

Prebaiting

On waters which have never seen boiled baits prolonged prebaiting will almost certainly be necessary before tench become conditioned to recognising them as food. They are much slower than carp in accepting anything new. Over a long period prebaiting need not be heavy, but with only a week or so larger quantities will probably be needed.

A number of anglers have said that boilies will not work on their water, but questioning reveals that they have gone about the business half-heartedly, putting only small amounts in. Liberal baiting is almost sure to work in due course, but some waters need longer than others.

Once tench are conditioned to accepting boilies, a change of flavour generally requires a much shorter period of prebaiting, often none at all. But that depends upon the quality of the base mix as well as the flavour.

Deciding how much to introduce during the session is a chancy game for there are so many variables. For instance, if you hope to intercept a small group of tench along a patrol bar it would be silly to saturate the spot because the bait with the hook in is liable to be overlooked. But larger holding areas like plateaux may need a more generous dose. Unless you suspect that other species are snaffling your pre-session baits there is little point in introducing more until you begin to get some action. It then pays to 'bait the bites', topping up with ten or twenty after every tench caught. Do that even if you miss the bite, working on the assumption that the missed tench will have cleared up a proportion of the free offerings.

Roll out the bait mix into long sausages, cut into sections, then roll between the palms of the hands.

Base Mixes

There is very little new in angling. Read this recipe from Richard Franck, who commended it in 1694:

Take fine bean flour, English honey, and poudred sugar, amalgamised or mingled with the yolk of an egg, and if the fat of an Heron be superadded to it, it makes it not the worse. Besides, sometimes he loves a taste of the dairy maid.

Information on the numerous ingredients with which to make base mixes is widely available in dealers' catalogues. They refer mainly to carp baits, but the principle of a bulk ingredient plus a binder is the same when considering tench baits. At one time I believed that the benefits of high-protein or HNV (high nutritional value) baits as used in some styles of carp fishing were inapplicable with tench. I thought that their catholic taste would call for nothing more than a cheap, easily mixed base, the ingredients of which had no great importance other than as a carrier for a good flavour. In some situations I still think this holds good, but in others I am satisfied that a good-quality base can be very important.

It really depends upon how long you plan to fish any one water. If you propose to fish a water only for the first week or two of the season, or merely for the odd day here and there, poor-quality bases will be adequate provided the flavour is good. Low-quality bases are also all that is needed during a long prebaiting phase on any water where boilies have not so far been used, though continued fishing there may call for a change to a better mix when bites begin to tail off, which they almost certainly will with hard fishing.

It is a good plan to make boilies in the close season for storage in the freezer, where they will keep fresh until needed.

Over a long fishing period on any one water a high-quality HNV base will out-fish a low-quality one. To really put this business of poor base versus HNV to the test, both mixes need to be used simultaneously over a long period on a selected water, one you know well and can fish regularly. I did exactly this over a full tench season. With one rod I used a low-quality carbohydrate mix consisting of 8 oz semolina and 4 oz soya flour plus two eggs (though semolina base mixes do not need eggs since they bind well without). On the other rod I used an HNV bait using 6 oz casein, 2 oz calcium caseinate, 2 oz lactal-bumen, 2 oz gluten, ½ oz vitamin mineral supplement and five eggs, giving an approximate 88 per cent protein balanced mix. Concentrated sweetener plus 10ml of butterscotch flavour was added to both. The carbohydrate baits were boiled for 30 seconds while the HNV, to get about the same hardness allowing for the different ingredients, was boiled for 75 seconds.

I prebaited before the season's opening, but thereafter further baiting was carried out only during fishing sessions. Baiting was indiscriminate – I scattered both baits at random so they overlapped around the general area fished.

Both rods were fished in the same area and rigged with identical terminal set-ups. At times they were adjusted to cater for the mood of the tench, but if I altered one the other was also adjusted. And to further ensure an unbiased experiment I periodically interchanged rod positions so that each bait was fished for about equal periods of time on both sides of the swims.

During the opening weekend I caught thirteen tench. Eight took the rubbish bait and five the HNV. The following weekend saw nine in the net, five on HNV and four on the rubbish bait. The third trip was a one-day session when I took six tench, three to each bait. So far, then, nothing to choose between them. And so it continued, until, around early August, I noticed a definite preference for the HNV bait, which began to outfish the other consistently.

By late August takes on the poor bait had tailed off further, and by late September had become a rarity. Circumstances then necessitated a lay-off for nearly three weeks, but on returning in mid-October I found it quite impossible to get anything other than odd tweaks on the rubbish bait, while I continued to catch consistently on the HNV right up until frosts made further tenching too slow to bother with.

Overall results: 107 tench to 6lb 5oz – 68 to HNV, 39 to RB.

You may say, 'So what? The results represent those of one angler on one water. Perhaps other waters and tench would respond differently.' Indeed they may, and I would be interested in findings elsewhere. But, conclusions after a day or a fortnight are of no use. Considering the variables of fishing conditions, any such project, to be meaningful, must be undertaken over a long period.

In the meantime, I have no plans to tackle any water, *long-term*, with any base other than a HNV.

Bait Consistency

Ever since the first boilie caught a tench I have argued that they are eaten despite their hardness not because of it; that given the choice tench actually prefer soft baits. Today I stand by that statement, which is now backed by considerable experience of fishing both baits side by side. Without exception I found that soft baits outfished hard. Soft baits have not been slightly better – they have been twice as good.

As I see it, some tench fishers are blindly emulating the success of carp men – who, remember, devised hard baits to deter unwanted species such as tench! The thick skin on hard baits seals in the flavour so they make even less sense when you consider that tench feed mainly by smell. All right, you can increase the flavour dose to compensate, but in doing so you are effecting a remedy for a problem which does not really exist.

If I am right, why is it that thousands of tench are being caught on hard boilies? Simply because they are there. Tench eat them because of their willingness to exploit any food if there is enough of it.

Hard baits produce incessant twitches and half-takes, while soft baits – of the same base and the same flavour, fished side by side with the hard – induce positive pulls. I used to believe that where a water was heavily baited with boilies I would be compelled to use them too because the tench would have become conditioned to accepting nothing else. I have changed my mind. On several such waters softies have still outfished boilies.

In advocating soft baits I do not mean paste, which is inconvenient because it is impossible to keep balls separate for catapulting other than by freezing them and taking them to the water in a flask, or by allowing paste balls to skin over in the sun. I give my baits a very light boil, just enough to form a skin to keep them separate. Boiling time varies with the mix, but from 15 to 30 seconds is enough for most.

Buoyant Baits

Rod mentions the effectiveness of buoyant baits – something I heartily endorse, having taken scores of tench by anchoring the bait to rise two inches off bottom. There are several ways to obtain the buoyancy: baking the baits after boiling, as Rod suggests (for which the wife's microwave oven is invaluable); using very light ingredients such as sodium caseinate and shrimp meal in the mix; or including a small chunk of polystyrene in the middle of a bait ball.

Tench usually need liberal baiting with boilies before they will begin to take them confidently.

Buoyant baits fished over a carpet of bottom baits are deadly.

A useful idea is to carry an emergency supply of dry ingredients along with a small bottle of flavouring to make buoyant baits at the waterside. Sodium caseinate is extremely buoyant and, mixed with a small proportion of wheatgerm, makes a superb floating paste. Bag it up dry at home and mix with a little lake water as needed.

Bait Size and Colour

I catch most of my tench on undyed baits which come out a pale or medium brown with the bases I use. But there are times when the addition of colours at the red end of the spectrum – yellows, oranges and reds – makes baits more effective, though I

tend to save them as trump cards for when bites tail off on ordinary baits. They do not *have* to be bright or pale colours to catch; softies based on molasses meal, which gives a dark colour, have proved very successful.

I think baits the size of a large garden pea or chick pea, about 8mm diameter, are perfect for tench. The snag is in the rolling and boiling of hundreds of little balls, surely the most tedious task ever devised. Prepacked ready-made boilies are available from dealers, albeit at the moment either too large or too small, but fortunately Rod's firm, Catchum Products, is soon to market a range of ready-made 8mm boilies specially for tench. I for one cannot wait!

Sweeteners

There is no doubt that tench like sweet baits. Mention has already been made of artificial concentrated sweeteners which are added to the bait in very small doses. However, because these are so highly concentrated, something like 200 times the strength of sugar, fish can easily identify them in a bait on which they have been caught, and learn to avoid further baits with the same sweeteners even if the flavour is changed. Changing to a natural sweetener may get things moving again, but it may be better to forget about any sweetener at all once the fish get wise to the artificial. A better strategy, I think, is to begin with natural sweeteners, which tench are less able to identify, leaving the highly concentrated stuff to fall back on. Caster and demerara sugar, honey, golden syrup and condensed milk can all be used.

SAMPLE RECIPES

HNV
6 oz casein
2 oz calcium caseinate
2 oz lactalbumen
2 oz gluten
½ oz Carpvit
10 ml flavour
1 ml concentrated sweetener
Approximate protein content 88%
Mix with eggs

Mid-protein
4 oz casein
2 oz sodium caseinate
2 oz wheatgerm
2 oz soya flour
2 oz caster sugar
10 ml flavour
Approximate protein content 60%
Mix with eggs

Fish-base
4 oz Pruteen
3 oz white fish-meal
2 oz shrimp meal
2 oz salmon fry
1 oz gluten
½ oz Carpvit
No flavour or sweetener

Molasses Base
5 oz semolina
4 oz molasses meal
2 oz soya flour
1 oz wheatgerm
No flavour or sweetener

Cheap Base Mix
8 oz semolina
4 oz soya flour
10 ml flavour
2 oz caster sugar

Multiples

Any identical items of bait, whether used in mass or in smaller quantities, come under the heading of multiples. Some – like maggots, casters, corn and wheat – have already been described in Chapter 15.

One of the attractions of multiples is the lack of preparation involved. Just soak and boil, and flavour if you like, and that is it. I have had less experience with these baits than others, but have to say that what fishing I have done with them has not really produced outstanding results. However, I have friends who swear by them, and I know of plenty of examples of tench going potty on one particle or another, and in extreme cases carp anglers have had to abandon a bait because tench refused to leave them alone. On a local syndicate lake one year every tench caught literally rattled after a prolonged prebaiting with black-eyed beans by the carp members.

Black-eyed beans have in fact proved to be the best particle bait, not only in my limited experience but in the experience of friends who use them more than I. Rod Hutchinson recommends flavouring them with tomato soup, and chicken stock cubes, Oxo and Bovril have also done the trick on other waters.

Chick peas have been successful for others but less so for me. Again, flavouring or dying or both are recommended to increase their attractiveness. Much the same can be said about any of the peas and beans. The problem when I have used them is not so much which to use but how much.

Dry Ingredients for Buoyant Paste
8 oz sodium caseinate
2 oz wheatgerm
Plus flavour

Baiting sparingly has failed to wean tench onto them even though others say they have instant results, while with liberal baiting I have had no trouble getting tench to accept them, but tiny bites have been the result. The tench become accustomed, as they do on any particle introduced in large quantities, to moving very short distances to suck in each piece, hardly registering a bite.

Bolt rigs cure the problem, but it is not a method I enjoy and for preference I would change baits. Scattering baits over a wider area works partly too, because the fish then have to move a bit further to find the next item. But widely scattered baits do not concentrate fish into a tight patch, which I prefer to do when I can.

From chatting to more successful particle anglers than me, it seems that the best way is to bait liberally for a week or two, but to cut down the feeding rate drastically before and during the fishing session, forcing tench to search and so to give better pulls. Even so, they all admit to lots of twitch bites too. Short of a finely adjusted antenna float rig and a fast striking arm, the problem remains.

Multiples have proved the answer on very rich waters where there is an abundance of natural food. In these waters tench can be so totally preoccupied that they are exceptionally difficult to tempt with ordinary baits. Small particles in quantity may in due course come to be accepted as part of their natural diet, and tench sometimes become preoccupied on them rather than on the natural food items.

Black-eyed beans, soya beans and boilies - all excellent tench catchers.

Hemp has proved to be one of the best baits for achieving this effect, but you make a rod for your own back because then tench become almost impossible to catch on any other bait than hemp itself. Good old crust may help if it is anchored just above the bottom, and strings of hemp grains mounted with a fine needle on to a hair rig have accounted for good catches for me in these situations.

17 · Groundbaits

Saturday evening, in my boyhood days, was groundbait-mixing night for my father, a keen angler in his day. All the leftovers of stale bread from my household, and from neighbours too, were dumped into the kitchen sink for overnight soaking, and the following morning, while the rest of the street slept, carefully squeezed free of surplus water, pulped to a slop between the fingers, and tightened with bran until a handful compressed nicely into a compact ball.

A hundred years before angling books were describing similar groundbaits for tench, and even today I know good anglers who still swear by this simple mix. Pulped stale bread breaks into an attractive milky cloud, the bran flakes dispersing to swirl freely about on the bottom, and both give a carpet of particles to entice tench into the area yet without overfeeding them. And therein lies the basic requirement of good groundbait – to attract the fish and stimulate them to remain and feed, but not to overfeed.

Binding Properties

Ideally a good mix 'explodes' just before or shortly after it hits bottom. I often see the advice that the bait should be mixed so that it breaks up on impact with the surface. This has merit over shallow swims, but over deeper water it encourages tench to rise to midwater to intercept falling particles, and while they can be caught off the bottom, they are easier

Jan Jefferson looks well pleased with her 4½lb tench.

when feeding hard on it, so that is where I want my groundbait to be.

What tench anglers do not want is hard lumps of uninviting stodge which thud to the bottom and just sit there without breaking up. Correct binding is as important, or even more so, than good ingredients. Generally the mix should be on the dry side rather than wet, and the best way is to mix all dry ingredients together then add them to the water – not the other way round, which never results in a uniform mix. Some ingredients increase in volume when wetted and this should be taken into account when adding the water. Aim for a damp, crumbly texture, leave the mix for fifteen minutes or so to swell, and then add a little more water to get it just right.

Test a small ball in the margins to see what happens. It should sink quite slowly, break up quickly as it touches bottom, and spread particles over a wider area as it does so. Swirl the water about to imitate the vortex which would be made by a powerful fin-wash of a tench; if the bait disintegrates, with lots of bits rising in suspension, the mix is right.

Ingredients

A list of the ingredients, smells and flavours I have experimented with would be a long one. Some of them did nothing for the mix, but a few emerged which I am sure increase attractiveness and may be incorporated into my mix depending on the fishing range and the binding properties wanted. Brown or white breadcrumb forms the usual bulk ingredient. Brown breaks up quicker than white and is more suitable for close range, while white is used whenever a tighter mix is required to hold together in flight for longer range.

I have incorporated layers' mash for many years, mainly for its smell, which tench seem to like, and for its powdery consistency, which helps to bind a dryish mix. Sausage rusk is a superb ingredient. It comes in several grades from fine powder to coarse grains, the latter being most useful. Rusk can be mixed to suit various purposes, depending upon how much water is added to it. Well wetted it increases to near twice its dry volume, needs a long standing period for absorption, binds tightly on its own, yet breaks up well on the bottom.

Dry rusk is very buoyant, and if less water is used a semi-buoyant mix results, which I like better. Coarse rusk grains are of different sizes so that some absorb less water than the rest and remain buoyant. If necessary I add dry rusk to a too wet mix to

Attractively scented groundbait mixes are important in tench fishing.

get the right effect. What happens in the water is that the semi-dry grains pop free from the ball as it breaks up, rising and falling again to create an area of particles moving about in suspension. Used in a feeder with enlarged holes to allow grains to pop clear, and with a small buoyant hook bait presented above, rusk is deadly.

Mix rusk too dry, though, and the balls of groundbait float, at least until enough water has been absorbed to sink them, and that can take some while, during which there is a steady rain of slowly sinking grains until the ball becomes waterlogged and sinks. Once the ball has sunk, the buoyant grains rise through the water as they are released, so you finish up with a steady rain of bits going up and others coming down. This certainly attracts fish, but it does induce tench to feed off the bottom, and as I have said they are generally easier to catch on it. A dry mix is also ineffective on a windy day – unless of course you want to bait up a swim fifty yards or so downwind. But rusk is excellent when thoughtfully used, and with or without crumb can form the basic bulk ingredient.

An ingredient in which I have great faith is an awful-smelling mixture called fish, blood and bone meal. At one time I used neat bone-meal and found it good, but having experimented with the former mixture over several years I think it is better, to the extent that I am not happy unless I have some in the mix. It has a shingly texture, and should therefore only be used in low quantities, or binding is difficult. The proportion can be increased for use at close range.

Ground hemp is another ingredient which definitely works. Cooked whole hemp seed is even better as an attractor, but, as I have said, it encourages preoccupation and twitchy tench. Ground hemp is only marginally less good, but does not preoccupy the fish. Trout pellets mixed in groundbait have worked well for friends, though I cannot seem to do much

Retain the yellow foot for the hook, use the rest of the mussel for the groundbait.

Harry Green prepares to return a brace of 6-pounders – something few anglers had experienced in the early seventies when this catch was made.

with them. There have been a few occasions when tench have responded to this groundbait used in conjunction with a paste made from pellets as hook bait. Salmon Fry powder used in both groundbait and hookbait is, I think, better, though I do not include such ingredients as standard additions. Overdoing additions leads to confusion; if the mix fails you do not know which to delete, and if it scores you cannot be certain which or how many did the trick. Better to keep it reasonably simple with one or two proven attractors.

Adding maggots, etc. to the mix is of course a well proven technique, though they obviously need to be compensated for with more binder such as layers' mash to stop the ball breaking up. Squatts have less tendency to break up a ball because they wriggle less, and in my view they are the best maggots for feeding anyway, since they do not creep out of sight beneath bottom debris, and they provide more individual items to keep tench browsing. Pinkies are a close second, but are livelier and need a good binder. If ordinary maggots are all that is available it is a good idea to scald them with boiling water before adding them to the mix. Put them in a sieve then just pour the water over them, which kills them instantly. Scalded maggots stretch, turn a paler colour and stay where they are put instead of crawling out of sight. It is usual to retain live ones for the hook, but occasionally scalded maggots have outfished' live ones.

While maggots are a great attractor, casters beat them hands down as a holding bait and are as good in groundbait as they are on the hook. They bind well so you can cram lots into the mix, either whole or crushed. Similar comments apply to chopped lobs which I rate highly and have dealt with in Chapter 15.

Groundbait Colour

Now and again I have seen tench skirt around the outside of a patch of pale-coloured groundbait, or feed gingerly, obviously agitated, on the fringes. This probably happens more often than is realised, because it is uncommon to be able to see what is going on below. Probably some of these fish, perhaps all, have been caught from a similar pale patch and have become wary of entering. If you suspect that this is happening – for instance, if you see lots of bubbling outside your baited patch – the remedy is to use a darker groundbait, preferably one with a different smell too. You could use edible dye and

flavour, but I have found that molasses meal fits the bill perfectly, an almost black tea-leaf-textured substance with a sweet smell and taste. I started to use it in the swims described but found it such a good addition in its own right that I recommend it anywhere.

Additives and Attractors

Even the old-time tench anglers loved to experiment with various additives, such as aniseed, tar, oil of rhodium and blood, all of which I have tried at one time or another. Aniseed has done nothing at all for hook or groundbait. Neither has tar, which is not ordinary tar, as many suppose, but a derivative of tree sap – a wood tar. This is powerful stuff, and half a teaspoon in a full bucket of groundbait stinks to high heaven. A few drops is enough (too much, perhaps, from a tench's point of view). If you want to try it, chemists may obtain it for you, and Duncan Kay's Bait Services had a whole tinful they would have been glad to get rid of!

GROUNDBAIT MIXES

Close Range
Bread and bran
20% molasses meal
5% ground hemp

Close Range
50% brown crumb
25% molasses meal
15% layers' mash
10% fish, blood and bone meal

Longer Range
40% white crumb
35% sausage rusk
15% fish, blood and bone meal
10% layers' mash

Longer Range
60% sausage rusk
20% white crumb
10% layers' mash
5% ground hemp
5% fish, blood and bone meal

Proportions are approximate and may need adjustment for good consistency, depending upon the amount of liquid used.

A close-range swim raking session. A long-handled rake throws further for longer range work.

An ageing gamekeeper once whispered in my ear the magical properties of oil of rhodium, and though I have not tried it often enough to give an expert opinion I do believe there may be something in it. Blood is an old ingredient, but was really highlighted by Fred J. Taylor and his brothers in more recent times when they took huge hauls of tench from Wotten Lakes whilst using it in their groundbait. Dried blood is freely available from garden centres, but while it seems to do no harm it seems to do little good either – except for perch and eels, which love it.

But Fred went the whole hog and chose blood straight from the slaughterhouse. Having obtained some and used it, once, I salute his stomach. While it was really fresh I just managed to avoid being sick, but the tray I saved to congeal as hook bait was, as far as I was concerned, untouchable. I caught tench well with the fresh stuff in the groundbait, but it really is awful to handle and, tench or no tench, I intend to leave it strictly alone from now on.

Finally, do not forget that a ball of soil, especially that from a molehill, can liven up an otherwise dead tench swim. And milk in groundbait, either powder, liquid, or condensed, clouds the water beautifully and is an attractor in itself.

18 · Winter Tench

Stillwaters

Carp anglers are nowadays so successful in winter, even in sub-zero temperatures, that people often speculate about the prospects for winter tench too. But tench are not carp. Carp anglers have found that a short feeding spell occurs on most waters at some time almost every day or night, but I am quite certain that this does not happen with tench, even that there are waters where they hardly feed at all throughout the winter.

During my more dedicated years I always continued tench fishing into late autumn until I was simply unable to catch any more, some years persisting well into winter proper. As water temperatures begin to fall steadily towards winter, tench feed for progressively fewer and shorter periods as their metabolism slows. Accordingly they become much harder to catch until at 52° Fahrenheit, usually in late October or early November, they virtually cease to feed. At least, over the number of years I tried, that was the lowest temperature at which I could catch them.

As temperatures drop further with the onset of frosts, tench become torpid on the bottom, virtually motionless, the only perceptible movement a slight pulsing of the gills. I do not believe that they burrow into mud, but that they settle in an area of lying weed which decays around and conceals them. Once I marked the position of one fish and kept an eye on it until, in due course, it was no longer possible to define its shape among the covering debris. Finally I thought it had gone so I poked the spot with a rod tip, bringing an eruption of silt and a disappearing tench tail.

However, that fish on the shallows was unusual. In most cases I think they retire to moderately deep weedy water. There are instances of tench being foul-hooked on spinners dragging the bottom in deepish water; one, from a Lincolnshire river, weighed over eight pounds.

The tench I poked with the rod departed in a hurry. Another which I saw in April lying almost buried in the liquid bottom silt of Beeston Lake in Norfolk allowed itself to be lifted to the surface on the blade of an oar before it awoke, only to waddle back to its former position.

These tench are in true hibernation. They remain in this condition until the water temperature stabilises at normal winter levels of about 40° to 44° Fahrenheit when they may again stir and feed, but sporadically and only in certain conditions. These feeding spells nearly always correspond with a protracted milder spell which raises the temperature a degree or two, and occur more reliably in waters with an inflow and outflow. In fact these waters are without any doubt the most reliable stillwaters for winter tench, especially if they have substantial feeder streams.

Opposite *Early February, snow-clad banks, but a taste of summer for the author with these two cold water river tench.*

Water movement is important. A sudden strong current following an influx of water after heavy rain encourages tench to move about, and once they are moving they become catchable.

Heavy rain in winter usually means nice mild spells and these opportunities are not to be missed since they are the best times of all. However, there are waters where temperature seems to have less effect on whether tench will or will not feed. Such waters have really strong-flowing feeder streams, giving a constant interchange of currents to keep tench active. Gosfield Lake in Essex is one water among others I can think of where a small river flows in one end and out the other, and where tench are consistently caught throughout winter regardless of weather. The feeders also have a slightly higher water temperature than stillwater, which no doubt is significant. Totally enclosed stillwaters, especially small ones, are in my view a complete waste of time which could be better spent after chub or pike.

Hard-bottomed waters are often cited as the best places in winter, but I suspect that this logic originates from fireside armchairs rather than from experience, and results from the assumption that hard bottoms would prevent tench burrowing into mud. As I have said, I do not believe that tench burrow into mud to hibernate, and anyway most hard-bottomed waters contain enough silt in the hollows for them to do so if they wished. Most good winter tench waters I know about are, on the contrary, soft-bottomed.

Apart from waters like Gosfield, feeding spells are much shorter than in summer, often taking place around midday and early afternoon, when water temperature may have risen a notch or two.

Location and Temperature Effects

In winter there is no weed, no bubblers and no rollers to give clues, and tench are moving about very much less, so finding them requires more persistence. 'In winter, fish the deepest holes,' they say, 'because the water there will be warmer.' But the well documented effects of winter on water temperatures suggest that this advice has limited value. Cold water is heavier than warm water, so as surface water cools it sinks, replacing the warmer bottom water which then rises to the top. (Anyone who takes a swim in a lake, even in summer, can feel the coolness on dangling legs compared with the warmth at the surface.) This circulation continues until there is a uniform 39·2° Fahrenheit throughout, at which water is at its heaviest. At that point a reversal happens, so that further cooling of the surface means that it no longer sinks, but floats on top of the heavier bottom layer at 39·2°. Even with ice on top the bottom water will not be lower than 39·2° Fahrenheit.

From this it is apparent that the deepest areas are indeed the warmest when the water has fallen below 39·2°, above which it is more likely to be warmer at the surface. But of course things are never quite that black and white in fishing. Strong winds, for instance, increase circulation, especially in shallow stillwaters, and largely cancel out the effects of stratification. Which is why you will usually find a uniform temperature from top to bottom in 5 or 25 feet of water in exposed lakes. On sheltered small waters the wind will have little circulation and in these the temperature may well be coldest at the bottom, at least until it cools beyond 39·2°.

There have been mild, windy days in

Gosfield Lake in Essex, where tench still feed despite winter temperatures.

winter when I have had good results in medium-depth swims facing the wind. The swims have been where thick weed grew in summer, particularly areas of decayed lily beds, and best results came when the mild spell occurred after a period of very cold weather. I believe in these cases the warmed-up surface water was blown into the fishing banks, turning under and giving a raised temperature from top to bottom in the medium-depth swims, in which tench were probably already resting because of the decayed weed there. If these conditions can be combined with the area of the outflow in those waters that have one, then you are in the pound seats for stillwater winter tench.

Rivers

The combined effects of slightly higher water temperatures and continual flow keep river tench far more active than those in stillwaters. From late autumn until temperatures bottom and stabilise there is a period when the fish are less inclined to move much, but even then they remain intermittently active enough to figure frequently in a river fisher's catch throughout the temperature range. Most are caught accidentally, for I know not a living soul who regularly fishes rivers deliberately for tench in winter.

Warm water discharges from power station outfalls provide tench fishing comparable to high summer, but the fishing is artificial and cannot be regarded as true winter tenching. Outflows apart, the

This lean 5lb 4oz tench accepted the author's boiled bait intended for carp in midwinter.

haunts of tench in rivers in winter are hardly different from those of summer – deeper slow runs, slacks (not eddies, which collect too much rubbish and have too much variation in current direction), the sides of mill pools and backwaters.

Once, I broke a hole in the ice covering a backwater of the Suffolk Stour to catch two tench before the hole froze over again. But that was exceptional, and it is as true on rivers as on stillwaters that prolonged mild spells offer the best conditions. Heavy rain which usually accompanies south and west winter winds provides ideal conditions because the extra push of water from pumping on drains or the opening of

river sluices stirs tench into more activity. In flood conditions tench will move into the shelter of backwaters out of the main flow, not necessarily deep ones either. I know of one real flood hotspot in a backwater no more than thirty inches deep, almost guaranteed to produce tench in a flood regardless of water temperature.

Baits and Tactics

The first significant discovery to be made by a winter tench fisher is that fine tackle, small baits, and careful presentation beat normal summer tactics by a long way. Floods are a notable exception; then, tench will engulf large baits like lobs and lob tails on substantial tackle, giving summer-like bites. But in more normal conditions tiny bites are to be expected, and delicate tackle is needed to register them.

Weed will have died, so the risk of a hooked tench running into danger no longer rules out light tackle. I like a 13 foot match-type rod with a snappy action to give a fast response to a small bite. Line strength is 2lb BS straight through to a size 18 or 16 hook, though I do not hesitate to use a finer hook length if that seems necessary. Losing tench through breakage even on such fine tackle is inexcusable in snag-free water. Just let a fish go where it likes and tire it by letting it bounce against the elasticity of the rod tip.

Not many tench enthusiasts venture out into snow, but these two river fish prove that it can be worthwhile.

As for bait, redworms stand above all others I have tried. They are the right size and – more important – keep wriggling even in very cold water, and I have found a moving bait essential. Failing reds, which are difficult to obtain in winter, small marsh worms are nearly as good, though I do not rate brandlings in winter or at any other time. Maggots which wriggle about in the bait box become inert in cold water, but are nevertheless a good winter bait despite their lack of movement. I have caught and I know others who have caught winter tench on flake, corn, boilies and other inanimate baits, but they are of limited use in winter.

When I have had enough to do it, loose feeding with reds or chopped marsh worms has proved effective, though loose-

fed maggots over a worm bait are also good. Feeding little and often, aiming for an almost continual sparse rain of items though the swim, usually provokes some response if tench are willing to feed at all, though it may require some persistence. A white cloud groundbait can also stir tench to investigate. Mix it with milk to enhance the cloud, and aim for it to break up at about two-thirds the depth of the swim to get an attractive cloud around the hook bait.

A point to remember is that a bait fished a few inches off the bottom gets more bites than one hard on. In near-static waters, like stillwaters and backwaters, a delicate antenna float rig presents the off-bottom bait well, and gives good indication of the characteristic small bites. With loose feeding it is not unusual for tench to rise in the water to intercept falling items, so space the shotting up the line to allow the bait to sink slowly. Bites on the drop are shown when the float fails to cock in synchronisation with the shot pattern.

Once the bait has settled bites are rarely signalled by more than a deliberate small dip or lift of the antenna tip, and it definitely pays to strike at anything, however slight. Most of the time a tiddler will be responsible, but suddenly the rod will buckle to a bite no different from all the others.

There has been some debate as to the fight of tench, and whether, like carp, they are at their heaviest in winter. Those I have caught, and others taken by friends, have shown a normal or slightly lower weight for their length compared with summer. None have appeared heavier than I would expect them to be in summer, which in any case is to be expected since, as I said at the beginning, tench are not carp. But let no one try to tell you winter tench do not fight!

PAST AND FUTURE

19 · Giant Tench

In a way, much of the mystery and intrigue has disappeared from tench fishing with the current bonanza of colossal fish being caught. At one time a 'double' was the talking point wherever keen tench men gathered together, an unattainable dream, always there but always just out of reach, speculated about and plotted against in hushed tones. The handful of anglers who had seen a double or knew of a water containing one were held in reverence, and he who had actually tangled with such a monster was regarded with awe.

Waters in which these leviathans had been spotted or hooked were cloaked in mystery – (magic names of the past like the Low Pond at Benniworth (code-named Woldale) where Maurice Ingham battled and lost, where John Ellis, always rational and realistic, spoke of tench with dorsals the size of the palm of a hand; Exton Park Lake, where Dick Walker saw, even hooked, tench of huge proportions only to lose them in dense lily roots; Castle Ashby, the home of doubles; the Revd Alston and the great tench of Ring Mere. Nostalgic stuff.

Recent big-tench history does nevertheless contain a sprinkling of giants which did find their way onto the bank, though not all by rod and line.

Early Records and Contenders

For a good many years the British tench record was jointly held by Mr Stacey, who captured one weighing exactly 7lb in 1882 from the Pottery Pits near Weston-super-Mare, and another of the same weight taken by the Revd E. C. Alston in 1933 from the Ring Mere at Wretham, near Thetford, Norfolk.

The Revd Alston's fish was particularly interesting in so far as he had actually stocked the water himself with about fifteen tench between 2½lb and 3lb. These tench came from nearby Standford Water, as did some fifty rudd to 1lb and a sprinkling of roach and pike, which he introduced along with the tench. Ring Mere was subject to fluctuating water levels, a factor which the Revd Alston believed to be a prime reason behind the subsequent phenomenal growth of the tench and rudd.

Time passed, and the first he knew of the success of his stocking was when a village lad caught a rudd going to 3lb 8oz. An experimental session produced what was, and probably still is, the most remarkable rudd catch on record, with some thirty fish between 2lb 4oz and 4lb 8oz, the latter holding the rudd record to this day.

The tench too had grown to enormous proportions. The 7lb fish with which he held the record was one of the smaller ones, and the monsters he saw to double figures were never taken despite news of his captures leaking out and the mere becoming heavily fished. The following summer the mere dried up and Alston went down with a landing net to save what he could. The tench, he said, were thin as rakes, weighing about 5 to 5½lb. He

Peter Tombleson of the British Record Fish Committee measures Alan Wilson's great tench. The length to the tail fork was 23½ inches.

saved some, along with some rudd to 2½lb, and a few small pike, which were moved to a nearby water.

The big tench scene was then quiet until, in 1947, a fish of 12lb was reputed to have been found in the margins of a lake at Burnham-on-Sea. The fish was not taken on rod and line and no substantiating evidence has been available.

On 10 July 1948 B.S. Dawson of Worthing caught a tench claimed to weigh 7lb 2oz and to measure 23 inches long by just over 17 inches in girth from a water near Chichester, Sussex, and entered it for the British record. The fish was taken to the famous taxidermists Cooper & Sons to

be mounted, but having examined it Coopers queried the claimed weight in a letter to the *Angler's News*, which controlled the record list at that time. Coopers said that the weight, upon receipt and in a frozen state, was found to be 6lb 2½oz – including the newspaper it was wrapped in – and suggested that a mistake may have been made with the original weighing.

The editor of the *Angler's News* invited Mr Dawson to take up the matter since their letter from him quoted the weight of 7lb 2oz along with witnesses to its weighing. Mr Dawson replied, and the result of the considerable investigations which followed – involving the *Angler's News*, the *Fishing Gazette*, the *Daily Mirror* and Bernard Venables (who was angling correspondent to that paper) – was that the weight originally claimed was accepted, and that Dawson's fish was the new record.

Despite the inaccuracies, I consider the measurements quoted entirely consistent with the claimed weight of 7lb 2oz.

However, it did not rule the roost for long. On the evening of August 1950, M. Foode, fishing a match on the Leicester Canal, struck into a tench of 8lb 8oz and in doing so well and truly shattered the previous record. Mr Foode took his tench on a piece of redworm, on a size 16 hook to 1½lb hook link, and did well to land the fish safely in twenty minutes in front of some twenty club witnesses.

As always, sceptics doubted the authenticity, believing it to be confused with a leather carp. But since the tench was returned alive that must remain unanswered. However, it does seem to me that while one angler, or even several, might conceivably confuse a tench with a leather it is hardly likely that twenty people including a water bailiff and the club secretary would all be wrong.

The Kennet Monster

One winter day, Sunday 11 February 1951, R. Blaber of Willesden, out for roach on a private stretch of the Kennet, caught what is still the second largest tench ever recorded in this country, a huge fish which dragged the scales down to 12lb 8oz. Mr Blaber noted that the fish was heavy with spawn, having a stomach distended 'almost to the size of a football'.

A spawny tench from a river in midwinter is unusual enough, but one of that size met with incredulity, especially since an hour later Mr Blaber hooked and subsequently lost after a long tussle a second tench which, judged from a sighting of its tail, was just as large as the first.

A claim was filed for the national record and, since the fish had been witnessed by three responsible anglers and the weighing scales certified correct, was duly accepted on 24 February by the *Angler's News*. But the country's anglers refused to accept this new record quite so readily. Sceptical letters began to arrive at the *Angler's News*. Some were highly suspicious of a tench which exhibited such a great increase over the current record, which at that time was still the 8lb 8oz fish taken by M. Foode. Some suggested that the fish might have been a carp; others voiced the opinion that February was a mite early for a tench to be distended with spawn, and that this abnormality could have been due to dropsy. The general feeling of scepticism also highlighted the question of claimed record fish being returned to the water. In fact, Blaber's tench sparked off reappraisal of the rules regarding record claims.

Meanwhile, the editors of the *Angler's News* remained silent until, on 28 July, they published the notable fish list for the 1950–1 season. Although Blaber's tench topped the list, an accompanying editorial entitled 'The Record Tench' stated that despite Blaber's conformation to all the rules the committee had decided that, since the tench had been abnormal, it could not be accepted as the new record, and that M. Foode's fish remained at the head of the list.

One reader summed it up in a letter which suggested that a 12lb 8oz tench weighs 12lb 8oz and, abnormality or not, it was a record fish.

Spawn or dropsy, no one will ever know for sure, because Blaber's great tench and the similar huge fish lost in the same session were never seen again. I think it very unlikely that the distended stomach was due to spawn, though it is remotely possible that the fish was spawn-bound and had failed to reabsorb the spawn by February. More likely the tench suffered from dropsy, the football belly distorted by several pounds of the fluid that this affliction creates.

More Giants

The next contender was a fish of 11lb from Wraysbury Pit in July 1959, the first tench ever taken by Donald Laing, a 17-year-old from Moor Farm, Wraysbury. It accepted legered bread flake. Photographs reveal that it also had a grossly distended stomach, the angler's hands literally holding it by the belly as one would a football.

Shortly after in the same year yet another Wraysbury giant was caught and entered for the record, this time a fish of 9lb 9oz 12dr. caught by Winston Dearsley. This latest fish, also of the football variety, was sent alive to the aquarium of the London Zoological Society, where it subsequently died. Meanwhile, the Zoological Society advised that the tench was suffering from an abnormal condition, following which the record committee ruled that 'it could not accept as a new record a tench which was abnormal, even though its rules did not cover this contingency'. Since the 11lb fish also suffered from this abnormality (presumably dropsy), that too was relegated.

1959 was a good year for big tench, with a further giant of 9lb 2oz reported from Wire Mill Lake in Surrey. The captor was Mr J. Parker from Kenley but no claim appears to have been made for the record.

In August of the following year, 1960, a Mr P. Martin of Chertsey claimed the capture of a tench weighing 9lb 3oz 4dr. from Chertsey Lake. However, this fish was never submitted for record status since it was returned to the water immediately to comply with the rules of the fishery.

So far much of tench record history is obscured by controversy. But not so the next fish, caught on 12 July 1963 by John Salisbury of Chatteris, Cambridgeshire, from Eggetts Lake at Hemingford Grey, Huntingdon.

Mr Salisbury had arrived early at the lake with his brother, and by 9 a.m. had taken a nice bag of fish to four pounds. His brother, fishing further round the lake, had been broken by heavy fish, so John lost no time in moving his tackle into the same area, where, baiting with red worms, he soon had a bite. The ensuing fight was long and hard, but in due course the fish slid over the rim of the net. It weighed 9lb 1oz.

This record was to stand until 1975, despite an unsubstantiated claim of a huge fish caught in the interim. On 13 August 1968 B. Wiseman of Kelveden reported a fish of 9lb 2oz, taken on bread from Rivenhall Lake in Essex. Although it was apparently weighed in the presence of two young witnesses, the tench slipped from his hands when he fell on the muddy banks, so no record claim was ever made.

During the opening week of the 1970 season Pete Pilley of Harrow landed a tench 22½ inches long by 19 inches in girth from a Middlesex water which, when first weighed, pulled the needle of the scales to 9lb 1oz 8dr. – half an ounce heavier than Salisbury's record. But within a short time its weight had gone down to 8lb 12oz after it had reportedly lost at least a pint of spawn, and so the tench was not submitted as a record. Pete was very unfortunate for, in all the years I have been tench fishing, I cannot recall an instance of a female losing spawn on capture, though I have heard odd reports of other fish doing so.

Tony Marris (left) and Les Millington of
The Tenchfishers Club with an 8lb and a
7lb tench respectively from a Cheshire
mere.

The First Double

Then came 1975, a momentous year for
tench enthusiasts everywhere for at last
the first authentic, healthy double-figure
tench was caught, and at 10lb 1oz 2dr. put
over a pound onto the former record. The
unassuming captor was Lewis Brown of
Peterborough, who had set up stall at 6.15
a.m. on Sunday 3 August at a brick pit not
far from his home, electing to fish on the
near shelf about one and a half rod lengths
from the bank.

His tackle was substantial – line 8lb BS
and hook size 6 – since Lewis knew well

enough that the pit contained some very
big tench indeed. Baiting with worm and
laying on with float tackle he missed two
bites, so he promptly changed to a small
section of worm. The result was a beautiful bite, followed by a five-minute tussle
and a few anxious moments before the
huge tench slid into the folds of his landing
net. Seeing the size of the fish, Lewis
dropped his rod and grabbed the net handle
with both hands, but it bent double under
the strain so net and tench were finally
dragged up the bank to safety.

After the capture Lewis told me not to
be surprised to see his record again toppled
by a larger fish from the same pit, but so far
his optimism has not been realised.

But things were happening fast in the
tench scene, as related in Chapter 7, and

although the seventies produced no more doubles there were several near misses with two fish of 9lb 11oz by R. Seal from Frimley Pit, Hampshire, and B. Blower from Pickmere, Cheshire, both in 1979. The following year also threw up a few close shaves with a tench of 9lb 13oz caught by an unknown angler reputedly from Hutton Rudby ponds near Middlesbrough, another nudging 9lb 8oz by Roy Ecob from Wilstone Reservoir at Tring, Herts, and one of 9lb 8oz 8dr. by Robert Taylor from Rugby.

The 1981 season began with a big bang, no less than three double-figure tench being reported in June. The largest came to the rod of Cheshire bream enthusiast Denis Kelly, and weighed 10lb 10oz. But Denis declined an attempt at a record claim. He caught the fish along with several others about 6lb on bunches of maggots to size 12 hook and 6lb line from a Cheshire mere. The huge tench, he said, was heavy in spawn and was quickly returned to the water to prevent unnecessary stress. It was, moreover, wrong in his view that a tench in that condition should be considered as a record.

The second largest double of 1981 at 10lb 4oz came to Richard Francis from the increasingly prolific big-tench water, Wilstone Reservoir. Unfortunately for Richard, however, his tench was foul-hooked in a ventral fin, and having checked with the British Record Fish Committee that a fish hooked outside the mouth was ineligible he made no claim.

Five days before, Tony Chester caught the 10lb 1oz 4dr. tench, the story of which he relates in this chapter, and in doing so pipped Lewis Brown's old record by just 2 drams.

Yet another superb double in the shape of a 10lb 2oz fish was netted by Eric Edwards from an Oxford gravel pit in June 1982.

Joe Darville also relates in this chapter how he was to become the next record holder with his 10lb 10oz tench caught in 1984 from an undisclosed Hertfordshire lake. Joe's fish was an old acquaintance of a few of the lake's regular anglers since she had been caught on several occasions in previous years at lower weights. Not that it detracts from the merit of the capture. Some of the heaviest tench on record are indeed repeat captures.

Recaptures

To digress for a while, it is at first glance logical to suppose that a tench, or any species, once caught, would be much harder to tempt a second time. This would apply particularly over a short period, before the fish had had time to forget the unpleasant experience of being caught. I believe, however, that exactly the reverse happens. A fish's way of life revolves around avoiding predation, breeding, and feeding, with the least amount of energy expended for the amount of food intake. An active fish with a high metabolism feeds more often and for longer periods because it has to replace the extra energy it is using. A fish which is hooked is obliged to use up tremendous reserves of energy during its struggle for freedom, sometimes, as we know, fighting to near-exhaustion.

Captured and returned fish need to replace all that lost energy, and they do it not only by resting but by more vigorous feeding. True, such a fish will also be more wary, but the food requirement negates much of that caution and the fish is very likely to be caught again quite quickly when its hunger prompts it to pick up another bait. And so begins a vicious circle: the more it gets caught the more it feeds, and the more likely it is to be recaught.

What I have said is speculation, but I have seen the same fish caught as many as seven times in a couple of months and friends quote similar examples. Often the fish being repeatedly caught is one which until the first capture had never been seen before.

But to return to the scene of giants, which has progressed to 1985, when it was announced to the angling world that Alan Wilson of Blackpool had blasted all previous records out of sight with a magnificent tench of 12lb 8oz, again from that stupendous big-tench fishery, Wilstone. Again, Alan tells his own story here and there is little to add but to wonder where the record goes from here.

Some Wilstone regulars, among them Bernard Double, the long-standing bailiff, believe that a yet larger tench is possible from the water. He talks of a 14lb fish as a distinct possibility. A few other large understocked waters, mainly gravel pits and reservoirs, could come up with the goods, and I too believe that we may yet see a pound or two added to Alan's record in due course.

The Thornville Tench

Although the tale has been told before, this narrative of yesterday's giants would not be complete without mention of the great tench of Thornville Royal. The Revd William B. Daniel first gave the account in his three-volume work published in 1801 entitled *Rural Sports*:

Its history is, that a piece of water at Thornville Royal, Yorkshire, which had been ordered to be filled up, and wherein wood, rubbish, etc., had been thrown for years was in November 1801 directed to be cleared out. Persons were accordingly employed, and almost choked up by weed and mud, so little water remained, that no person expected to see any fish, except a few eels; yet nearly 200 brace of tench of all sizes, and as many perch were found. After the pond was thought to be quite free, under some roots there seemed to be an animal, which was conjectured to be an otter; the place was surrounded, and on opening an entrance among the roots, a tench was found of most singular form, having literally assumed the shape of the hole, in which he had for many years been confined.

His length, from fork to eye, was 2 feet 9 inches, his circumference almost to the tail, was 2 feet 3 inches, his weight 11lb 9oz 4dr., the colour was also singular, his belly being that of a charr, or a vermilion. This extraordinary fish, after having been inspected by many gentlemen, was carefully put into a pond, but either from confinement, age, or bulk, it at first merely floated, and at last, with difficulty, swam away. It is now alive and well.

Even in those days, anglers were not slow to voice doubts about the authenticity of Daniel's tale, and it received a fair amount of ribbing, including the following verse:

> The scullion wench
> Did catch a tench
> Fatter than Berkshire hogs, Sir,
> Which pretty soul,
> Had made his hole,
> Snug shelter'd by some logs, Sir!
> Sans water he,

Had lived d'ye see,
Beneath those roots of wood, Sir!
And there alack
Flat on his back,
Had lain since Noah's flood, Sir!

Ribbing and the fact that many notable anglers consider it authentic aside, the tale does have fanciful tendencies and discrepancies. Daniel quotes the length as being 33 inches, while the caption to the engraving produced in *Rural Sports* and reproduced here quoted the length as 2 feet 3 inches.

Daniel's figure of 33 inches, together with the quoted girth of 27 inches put the fish within the realms of mermaids, because any tench with those dimensions could not weigh less than 20-plus pounds at least. The caption figures of 27 inches in length by 27 inches in girth is more credible, but still several inches more both ways than what I would expect the measurements of an 11lb 9oz tench to be.

In fairness to the reverend gentleman, however, it is probable that he obtained his information from the well-known figure of Colonel Thornton, whose home was Thornville Royal, and who, in due course, himself came under scrutiny when in 1805 he wrote a book of his angling adventures in Scotland, in which he claimed to have caught perch of over 8lb from Loch Lomond, and a pike near to 50lb.

Dreams Come True

It is one thing to dream of 'doubles', but

The famous tench of Thornville Royal.

quite another to have actually caught one. Here are the stories of three anglers who have no need to dream.

My Record TONY CHESTER

I had always been a stickler for local waters until a friend took a 7lb 9oz tench from Wilstone. The following year, 1980, saw both of us on the bleak reservoir banks, where we spent a week fishing the 'poplars' end. That week proved that the water held bigger fish than we thought possible, since my mate took one of 9lb 6oz. I blanked.

We returned a couple of weeks later but the fish had spawned and none were caught. These events led to my return on 14 June 1981 along with two friends, Roy Ecob and Dick Wollaston. We all arrived at about 7.15 a.m., climbed the steep side of the reservoir and looked toward the poplars. Just one bivvy in sight – not as crowded as we thought it would be after the 9lb 6oz fish of last year.

After the usual four or five trips carting gear to the swims we introduced ourselves to our new companion, Lester Strudwick, and within a couple of hours we were all shipshape, bivvies up and gear stowed neatly inside. The afternoon of the fifteenth saw eight rods resting in their usual cradles, ready for midnight. Mine were rigged for legering, one with a Drennen feeder for maggots, the other with a link leger for lobs.

The only thing left to do was to feed the swims, one with groundbait and chopped lobs, the other with groundbait and maggots. We decided to wait until about 9.30 p.m. before baiting the swims, giving the fish time to settle down before the magic hour. We all had that gut feeling of excitement and expectation that only anglers awaiting the off feel. Three pounds of groundbait plus lobs were put into a near swim and the same amount of groundbait mixed with maggots in a farther one.

At midnight the usual frenzied casts were heard – mine included. Optonics could be heard all over as everyone adjusted their bobbins. That first morning was disappointing, with only one fish of 6lb 9oz falling to Roy Ecob. We fished until about lunch time but to no avail.

After a bite and a pint at the pub it was back to the bivvy for a kip. The alarm clock woke us at 7 p.m., after which we rebaited the swims, ate, and settled once more for the night. At about 12.45 a.m. Lester, whose bivvy was to my left, hooked into a fish. I quickly got down the six-foot-high wall to the water's edge with the landing net, and slid it under the fish, which at first I thought was around the six or seven pound mark, but on lifting it I was amazed at the weight. I passed the net to Lester and clambered back to the top of the wall. The net was steaming as we all stood over it in the cool night air. When the mesh was unfolded there lay the second largest tench I had ever seen, which when weighed made 9lb 2oz – Lester's personal best and another man's dream realised at wonderful Wilstone.

But the next few days were to be the most rewarding of my own angling life. We had only just returned to our bivvies when I had a lovely bite. A firm strike sank the hook into my first Wilstone tench. It felt good. Lester was at the waterside in a flash with the net, and after a spirited fight he netted the tench for me. She looked perfect as she lay there in the torchlight, my largest tench at 7lb 3oz. I was ready to go home there and then!

You can imagine my feelings when an hour later the bite alarm sounded again.

This fight lasted about four minutes, and again Lester did the honours. And there lay an enormous tench. Someone muttered that it was definitely a nine-pounder but could even be ten pounds. We all laughed nervously, staring at its yellow flanks glistening in the torchlight. The weight was checked on two sets of Avons and found to be 10lb 2oz.

What to do next was the question. I slid her into my keepnet while we debated the situation, in the end deciding to report it to the angling press and apply to the BRFC for a record. I rang my wife to tell her the good news, then hurried to see the water bailiff, Bernard Double, who congratulated me and even seemed as pleased as I was. What a fantastic day!

My Record JOE DARVILLE

Ever since I started fishing for tench, particularly big tench, I have had good years and bad years, and some in-between years. 1984 started off rather slowly with only one fish taken in the first week, weighing 6lb 8oz, a good fish but nothing to get excited about. I did not realise that this slow start would develop into my best tench year ever, with the fish of 10lb 10oz and my best brace of fish at 8lb 4oz and 8lb 3oz.

On the day I caught the record fish the weather was diabolical, with the rain teeming down and a strong westerly wind. I've had more big tench in weather like that than in all the so-called 'tench fishers' dawns', but this time I drew a blank. As the evening drew near the wind gradually died down and finally dropped, and shortly afterwards the rain too eased and finally

Opposite *Tony Chester with his historical tench from Wilstone Reservoir, at 10lb 1oz 4dr. the former British record.*

stopped. It got warmer and quite muggy, and by six o'clock had become oppressive.

I decided to recast with fresh baits. I was fishing a bar about three rod lengths out, the top of which was about three feet deep and clear of weed. At the bottom of the bar it was ten feet deep with a considerable amount of short covering weed. I was fishing two rods and my right-hand bait, a high-protein paste, was resting on top of the bar, while the left-hand bait, a large lobworm with its nose nipped off and slightly injected with air to keep it resting on top of the weed, was placed at the bottom of the bar. I was using 11-foot carbon rods, Cardinal 54 reels, 6lb BS line and size 6 Jack Hilton hooks. The end rigs were straightforward link legers with swivels for stops.

Having cast out, I sat back to have a brew up. I was fishing a small picturesque pit surrounded by plenty of trees and bushes, very rich in bird and insect life. I lay back on the bed-chair, thought about the bait and methods I was using and wondered if a change would bring results. Suddenly the left-hand Optonic sounded and line began to trickle slowly off the spool. I leapt off the chair, grabbed the rod, flicked the bail arm over and struck. The rod slammed over as I connected with a heavy fish, which took off with the unmistakable heavy pull of a female tench. After three or four slow runs I drew the fish into the bank and as it slid over the net I thought, 'at last a nine-pounder'.

As I weighed it I stared in disbelief as the needle steadied on 11lb 3oz. I knew the weigh-sling weighed 9oz, which made the fish an incredible 10lb 10oz. I could hardly believe it. I weighed it again, counting the pounds as the needle went round the scales. It was right! The needle again stopped on 11lb 3oz. I was shaking like a leaf; at last I

had broken the tench record. I weighed the sling again and confirmed it at 9oz. The tench looked quite old; all its fins and tail had old splits in them and its mouth was torn from an old wound. It was only 21½ inches long and of a very dark colour.

I quickly sacked it and managed to contact my friend Steve Howard, who in turn contacted three other witnesses. Steve was first to arrive at my swim to find me still sitting shaking on my bed-chair. The other three arrived and together with Steve witnessed the weighing again and took photographs.

There followed a short discussion on whether I should claim the BRFC or the NASA record, eventually deciding on the latter since all they required was a photo of the fish and the word of the four well-known Lea Valley anglers, and I did not wish to retain the fish any longer than need be. Having made this decision, I returned the great fish to the water, and we watched in silence as it swam slowly back into deep water and out of sight.

The rest of the evening passed in a blur. It still had not sunk in that I had caught a record fish. I thought of all the years I had been after big tench and the long, sometimes lonely sessions, the different baits and methods I had used, some with success, and some not. It had all been worth it.

I caught one more fish that session weighing 6lb, rather an anticlimax, but it made a good double. NASA accepted my claim and I held the record for a year, until it was broken by Alan Wilson's fantastic fish.

Who knows, maybe I'll do it again some day.

My Record   ALAN WILSON

I arrived at Wilstone reservoir on 23 June 1985 well in time to get all the tackle and other gear needed for a longish stay into my chosen swim, one I had already had quite a bit of success in, taking a personal best fish of 9lb 6oz the previous year.

The reservoir looked beautiful and, with the westerly wind blowing into my swim, I knuckled straight down to the task of getting my gear round – quite a job, I can tell you. Having dumped the first lot and returned to the car I saw that Tony Chaffey from the Isle of Wight had arrived. I had met Tony last year when we fished for the bream together so we put the kettle on and sat down for a chat.

Tony asked me which pitch I fancied, to which I replied that there was only one place for me, and that was on the 'point', as we called it. I invited him to join me there, Tony accepted, and with that settled we got the boat in order to locate a submerged fence which we knew ran along a big bar adjacent to the point. My strategy was to locate the ends of the fence and place markers there so that I could cast up its sides without getting snagged. This took longer than I anticipated because the water level had risen and there was quite a chop on with the stiff wind.

The next job was to get the groundbait in, so I mixed nearly a bucketful of breadcrumbs with a tin of sweetcorn, forty or fifty lobworms, and about a pint of maggots, which were scattered along the side of the bar and the fence with the aid of the boat. My tackle comprised 11-foot carbon rods of 1¼lb test curve, and Cardinal 55s loaded with 8lb BS Maxima. I intended to try lobworm and maggots on the hook while Tony was to try lobworm and sweetcorn.

Britain's best by far: 12lb 8oz 11dr. of stupendous tench for current record holder Alan Wilson.

It was about 9 p.m. on Sunday evening by the time all was set up and we were ready to start. Two bites just before dark resulted in two bite-offs, both from little jacks that grabbed the worms, but nothing on the maggots or the sweetcorn yet. With darkness we decided to get our heads down as it is very rare to get action at night at Wilstone. But June nights are short and by 3.30 a.m. the sky is beginning to lighten. The first job of the morning, the compulsory cup of tea. Just after first light Tony also got bitten off, then it was my turn. These pesky pike must have been starving. But then Tony had a nice slow lift on corn, struck, but missed it. With that I switched

to corn myself, nicking two grains on a size 10 hook and placing it tight up to the side of the fence in about nine feet of water.

At 6.10 a.m. the indicator on the corn rod flickered into life and climbed deliberately to the butt ring. My strike brought a big thump on the other end. 'Is it a tench?' asked Tony. 'Don't know yet,' I replied; 'with all these pike about it is difficult to tell.' He came over with the net, but after about five minutes went back to tend to his own tackle. At this point I was still trying to keep the fish out of the fence, gaining a bit and then losing it. After seven or eight minutes I had it halfway back when it took off in a really determined run for the fence, and was I thankful for the 8lb line, because I had to clamp down hard and only just turned the fish away from danger at the last minute.

In all this time we still had not seen the fish, but I had it boring deep down and swimming round in big circles close in front of us. Then I saw it for the first time. 'At least it's a tench, and not a bad one,' I said to Tony. It set off in further deep, short runs, but at last began to tire, giving us a better look at it, which revealed that it was much bigger than I originally thought. By now Tony was ready with the net so I gently brought the fish closer. But it saw it and was off again, forcing me to give line. When I played it back for the second time the fish was well beaten and on its side, and came slowly over the rim of the net. For an anxious moment it balanced on the rim but finally slid into the mesh.

Climbing back up the steep bank sides at Tring with one hand, a big landing net and a big fish clutched in the other, is not easy. But between us we managed to get fish and netsman back to the top. Tony carried the fish to a nice soft grassy place to unhook it. As he was unfolding the mesh his exact words were 'Now what have we got here?' We put the fish into the weigh-bag, hooked it onto the scales and hoisted it up. 'Your scales are broken!' said Tony. 'They were all right last week,' I replied. So we tried it again, slowly this time, while Tony began counting the revolutions of the needle. 'Eight, nine, ten, eleven, twelve.' I thought, when is he going to stop?

But the needle on the Avon was indeed hovering between 12lb 8oz and 12lb 9oz, and with that I gave an almighty whoop of delight. I fished on, but without concentration, my mind still going over the events of the last half-hour. It still is!

20 · The Future

With some species notably in decline, the outlook for tench fishers nonetheless looks optimistic. In all but isolated regions the quality of tench fishing, far from declining, has got noticeably better, not only for big fish but throughout the size range.

Even the combined evils of abstraction and pollution in rivers, spelling doom to other fish, have in a way benefited tench fishers because the diminished flow and lack of competitors provide more ideal habitats for tench to thrive in. And, as I have already noted, tench in lowland rivers are certainly on the increase.

Tench of course have long been known for their resilience against adverse conditions, able not only to survive but actually to thrive in waters so low in oxygen or so poor in quality that few other species except eels are present. Even eels succumb before tench. In one lake years ago some fool dumped several half-full containers of chemicals into the water. Thousands of fish perished, and I watched sickly eels thrusting their heads out of the margins in an attempt to escape the filth. Of the considerable tench stocks not a single one was found dead; indeed, the tenching if anything got better.

Neither are tench vulnerable to the parasites and diseases which can seriously afflict weaker species. In forty years' fishing it is difficult to recall more than a mere handful which were not healthy, well-conditioned fish. Their adaptability and tendency to look after themselves with minimal fishery management must cer-

tainly be a major consideration in any stocking programme.

One indecisive area for the future of tench lies in the projected stocking of waters with grass carp. Tench and weed are synonymous, not only for the shelter weed provides but because of the food it contains, on which tench rely for their existence. Stocking a species that denudes the water of weed will ultimately lead to a decline in the tench in that water. There are no maybes about it; tench would decline.

Scientists tell us that other fish species, bream in particular, feed on the faeces of grass carp and show increased growth. But tench are not bream. They also assure us that grass carp cannot breed in the water temperatures of our country, and so selective stocking with just a few would control but not eradicate the weed. I am certainly dissatisfied with those statements; it was impossible for rainbow trout to breed here but they do, in some places. And in the freak temperatures experienced in a summer like 1976 there is reason to believe that grass carp might well reproduce.

Anglers *must* be consulted fully before even one of these aliens is introduced.

Specialist Organisations

THE TENCHFISHERS

Over thirty years ago a small band of anglers gathered together with the object of forming a specialist group of tench enthusiasts, dedicated to the pursuit of

Tench fishers can well do without excessive weed clearance.

larger than average tench. The gathering was a veritable who's who of fishing at the time – Fred J. Taylor, John Ellis, Maurice Ingham, John Roberts, Frank Murgett, Norman Woodward and, later, Dick Walker. At the close of the meeting the Tenchfishers Club was born.

It operated basically by means of a rotary letter in which each member commented on some aspect of tenching before passing the letter to the next member for continuation of the discussion. Thus knowledge was pooled for the benefit of all. The idea worked for a while, but rotary letters, while they are superb vehicles for discussions between people who are unable to meet frequently, are notoriously slow to circulate, so discussions may no longer be topical by the time the letter reaches a member. So the impetus died, and the original Tenchfishers, while not disbanding, in due course became inoperative.

And so the club slept until, in 1967, it was reborn after discussions between the former founder member John Ellis and Dr Terry Coulson. Within a short time some forty single-minded tench enthusiasts had joined from all parts of the country, including yours truly. Under John's administration as secretary and Terry's scientific guidance as president, the club embarked upon ambitious projects designed to accumulate large amounts of data from the recorded fishing results of its members. Almost every aspect of tench fishing was recorded and quantitatively analysed – eventually, it was hoped, to be interpreted into tench-fishing facts.

Before long the mass of accumulated

data, despite the use of a computer (a novel idea at the time), looked in danger of overwhelming the time and resources for analysis. At the same time some members began to question the feasibility of the scientific analysis of angling data, expressing the view that variables in fishing made nonsense of quantitative interpretation. To obtain meaningful results from the various recording projects 100 per cent support from the membership was essential, and because that was no longer evident Terry and John in due course resigned.

And so, in 1972, the club again faltered. However, under the chairmanship of Ed Foottit and with myself as secretary it embarked on a less ambitious and more general approach to tench fishing. The rotary letter recommenced, a bulletin circulated regularly, various recording projects were continued and a regional structure was formed to facilitate localised projects and closer contact between members.

Today the club flourishes. Membership still numbers about forty, though applications from serious tench enthusiasts are welcomed. The reconstituted Tenchfishers are now in their twentieth year, and although I relinquished membership several years ago I have warm memories of having shared in the formative years. Since their combined knowledge is made available through occasional articles to tench anglers everywhere, I think we should all wish them continued success.

THE NATIONAL ASSOCIATION OF SPECIALIST ANGLERS

If the Tenchfishers are background ambassadors, NASA is surely the modern anglers' watchdog, not only for tench but for all freshwater fish. NASA is constituted to campaign on all anglers' behalf for an angling environment in which fish can live in optimum conditions for health and growth. Of all national organisations I feel NASA stands alone in unbiased representation of the general angler. It is answerable to no one but its membership, which increases by leaps and bounds. Perhaps NASA is best known for its annual British Angling Conference – a highlight of the year for hundreds. Other areas of activity include the development of an anglers' fighting fund, the proceeds of which in due course will be directed towards opposing the anti-angling lobby and promoting the anglers' image as the conservationists they are. NASA is also at the forefront of actions protesting against the deterioration of some of this country's finest fisheries. As tench lovers I believe that all my readers ought to subscribe to its cause.

THE ANGLERS' CO-OPERATIVE ASSOCIATION

The ACA was founded thirty-eight years ago as a non-profit-making organisation dedicated to fighting water pollution. Like NASA, it does not exist solely for the protection of tench waters but encompasses all fisheries. Here is another voluntary organisation, manned by people of immense dedication, fighting pollution and existing solely on the subscriptions and donations of its members who, considering the numbers of clubs and individual anglers in this country, are pitifully few. What if that lovely lily-fringed tench lake received a lethal dose of silage? How would a club get compensation from the originators of industrial effluent which got into the feeder stream of their tench pond? The

Opposite *One of the early stalwarts of The Tenchfishers, Dick Ongley, nets a boat caught fish from Loblay Pound in Warwickshire.*

ACA has experts in the field of law and freshwater biology to present such cases, and has a quite unique record of success in obtaining redress for its members. The support of the ACA by all tench anglers will help to ensure the future prosperity of the species.

Conclusion

Nowadays the opinion is often expressed that in order of popularity with anglers tench come third behind carp and pike. I question that opinion, which I think is based upon the numbers who actually specialise in those species. Taking the angling fraternity as a whole, it appears that over the course of a season many never actually fish for carp, and to a lesser extent the same applies with pike. But there are very few who do not, at some time between June and September, find themselves on the banks of some weedy pool, intently watching a dithering float tip which, any moment, will surely slide away as a tench below sucks in the bait.

Index